S0-BRS-140

SOUTH PACIFIC

.—.o(}o.—.

SOUTH PACIFIC

A MUSICAL PLAY

MUSIC BY
Richard Rodgers

LYRICS BY
Oscar Hammerstein, 2nd

BOOK BY
*Oscar Hammerstein, 2nd,
and Joshua Logan*

ADAPTED FROM
*James A. Michener's
Pulitzer Prize-Winning*
TALES OF THE SOUTH PACIFIC

RANDOM HOUSE NEW YORK

M
1503
R684
S6
30241

COPYRIGHT, 1949, BY
RICHARD RODGERS AND OSCAR HAMMERSTEIN, 2ND
COPYRIGHT IN CANADA, 1949, BY
RICHARD RODGERS AND OSCAR HAMMERSTEIN, 2ND

FIRST PRINTING

The photographs in this book are by John Swope

NOTE: *Any reproduction or performance of this play or the music thereof, in whole or in part, is an infringement of copyright and is prohibited unless expressly authorized in writing by the authors and composer*

All rights reserved under International and Pan-American Copyright Conventions

Published in New York by Random House, Inc., and simultaneously in Toronto, Canada, by Random House of Canada, Limited

MANUFACTURED IN THE UNITED STATES OF AMERICA

Q.B.

To our patient Dorothy and Nedda, who liked it even when all the parts were sung and acted by us.

SOUTH PACIFIC *was first produced by Richard Rodgers and Oscar Hammerstein, 2nd, in association with Leland Hayward and Joshua Logan, on April 7, 1949, at the Majestic Theatre, New York City, with the following cast:*

(IN ORDER OF THEIR APPEARANCE)

NGANA	Barbara Luna
JEROME	or { Michael De Leon Noel De Leon
HENRY	Richard Silvera
ENSIGN NELLIE FORBUSH	Mary Martin
EMILE DE BECQUE	Ezio Pinza
BLOODY MARY	Juanita Hall
BLOODY MARY'S ASSISTANT	Musa Williams
ABNER	Archie Savage
STEWPOT	Henry Slate
LUTHER BILLIS	Myron McCormick
PROFESSOR	Fred Sadoff
LT. JOSEPH CABLE, U.S.M.C.	William Tabbert
CAPT. GEORGE BRACKETT, U.S.N.	Martin Wolfson
CMDR. WILLIAM HARBISON, U.S.N.	Harvey Stephens
YEOMAN HERBERT QUALE	Alan Gilbert
SGT. KENNETH JOHNSON	Thomas Gleason
SEABEE RICHARD WEST	Dickinson Eastham
SEABEE MORTON WISE	Henry Michel
SEAMAN TOM O'BRIEN	Bill Dwyer
RADIO OPERATOR BOB MC CAFFREY	Biff McGuire
MARINE CPL. HAMILTON STEEVES	Jim Hawthorne
STAFF SGT. THOMAS HASSINGER	Jack Fontan
SEAMAN JAMES HAYES	Beau Tilden
LT. GENEVIEVE MARSHALL	Jacqueline Fisher
ENSIGN DINAH MURPHY	Roslyn Lowe
ENSIGN JANET MAC GREGOR	Sandra Deel
ENSIGN CORA MAC RAE	Bernice Saunders
ENSIGN SUE YAEGER	Pat Northrop
ENSIGN LISA MINELLI	Gloria Meli
ENSIGN CONNIE WALEWSKA	Mardi Bayne
ENSIGN PAMELA WHITMORE	Evelyn Colby
ENSIGN BESSIE NOONAN	Helena Schurgot
LIAT	Betta St. John
MARCEL, Henry's Assistant	Richard Loo
LT. BUZZ ADAMS	Don Fellows

Islanders, Sailors, Marines, Officers: Mary Ann Reeve, Chin Yu, Alex Nicol, Eugene Smith, Richard Loo, William Ferguson

BOOK AND MUSICAL NUMBERS STAGED BY Joshua Logan
SCENERY AND LIGHTING BY Jo Mielziner
COSTUMES BY Motley
ORCHESTRA DIRECTED BY Salvatore Dell'Isola
ORCHESTRATIONS BY Robert Russell Bennett

*The action of the play takes place on two islands in the South
Pacific during the recent war. There is a week's lapse of time
between the two acts.*

MUSICAL NUMBERS

ACT ONE

Dites-Moi Pourquoi	Ngana and Jerome
A Cockeyed Optimist	Nellie
Some Enchanted Evening	Emile
Bloody Mary Is the Girl I Love	Sailors, Seabees, Marines
There Is Nothing Like a Dame	Billis, Sailors, Seabees, Marines
Bali Ha'i	Bloody Mary
I'm Gonna Wash That Man Right Outa My Hair	
	Nellie and Nurses
I'm in Love with a Wonderful Guy	Nellie and Nurses
Younger Than Springtime	Cable
Finale	Nellie and Emile

ACT TWO

Soft Shoe Dance	Nurses and Seabees
Happy Talk	Bloody Mary, Liat and Cable
Honey Bun	Nellie and Billis
You've Got to Be Taught	Cable
This Nearly Was Mine	Emile
Reprise: Some Enchanted Evening	Nellie
Finale	

ACT ONE

ACT ONE

SCENE I

SCENE: EMILE DE BECQUE's *plantation home on an island in the South Pacific.*

On your right as you look at the stage is a one-storied residence. On your left is a teakwood pagoda at the edge of the cacao grove. House and pagoda are bordered and decked in the bright tropical colors of the flaming hibiscus, the purple bougainvillaea, and the more pale and delicate frangipani. Between the house and the pagoda you can see the bay below and an island on the open sea beyond the bay. Twin volcanoes rise from the island.

AT RISE: *As the curtain rises, two Eurasian children,* NGANA, *a girl about eleven, and* JEROME, *a boy about eight, are, with humorous dignity, dancing an impromptu minuet. A bird call is heard in the tree above.* JEROME *looks up and imitates the sound. The eyes of both children follow the flight of the bird.* NGANA *runs over to the pagoda and climbs up on a table and poses on it as if it were a stage.* JEROME *lifts his hands and solemnly conducts her as she sings.*

NGANA

Dites-moi
Pourquoi
La vie est belle,
Dites-moi

3

Pourquoi
La vie est gai!
Dites-moi
Pourquoi,
Chère mad'moiselle,
Est-ce que
Parce que
Vous m'aimez?

> (HENRY, *a servant, enters and scolds them.*)

HENRY

Allez-vous! Vite! Dans la maison!

NGANA

Non, Henri!

JEROME

> (*Mischievously delivering an ultimatum*)

Moi, je reste ici!

HENRY

Oh, oui? Nous verrons bien . . . (*He chases* JEROME *around the giggling* NGANA) Viens, petit moustique!

> (HENRY *catches* JEROME. *He is not as angry as he pretends to be, but he grabs* JEROME *by the ear and leads him off squealing, followed by* NGANA, *who protests violently.*)

NGANA

Non, Henri . . . non . . . non!

> (*As she runs off,* NELLIE *and* EMILE *are heard offstage from around the corner of the house.*)

NELLIE'S VOICE

What's this one?

EMILE'S VOICE

That is frangipani.

NELLIE'S VOICE

But what a color!

EMILE'S VOICE

You will find many more flowers out here.

(NELLIE *enters, looking around her, entranced by the beauty of the scene. She turns upstage to gaze out over the bay.* HENRY *comes on from downstage with a tray which he takes over to the coffee table.* EMILE, *entering a few paces behind* NELLIE, *comes down briskly and addresses* HENRY.)

EMILE

Je servirai le café.

HENRY

Oui, Monsieur.

EMILE

C'est tout.

HENRY

Oui, Monsieur de Becque.

(HENRY *exits.* NELLIE *comes down, still under the spell of the surrounding wonder.*)

NELLIE

Well, I'm just speechless! . . . And that lunch! Wild chicken— I didn't know it was ever wild. Gosh! I had no idea people lived like this right out in the middle of the Pacific Ocean.

EMILE
(*Pouring coffee*)

Sugar?

5

NELLIE

Thanks.

EMILE

One?

NELLIE

Three. (EMILE *smiles*) I know it's a big load for a demitasse to carry. All right, I'm a hick. You know so many American words, do you know what a hick is?

EMILE

A hick is one who lives in a stick.

NELLIE

Sticks. Plural. The sticks.

EMILE

Pardon. The sticks. I remember now.

NELLIE

How long did it take you to build up a plantation like this?

EMILE

I came to the Pacific when I was a young man.
(NELLIE *studies him for a moment.*)

NELLIE

Emile, is it true that all the planters on these islands—are they all running away from something?

EMILE

(*Pausing cautiously before he answers*)
Who is not running away from something? There are

6

fugitives everywhere—Paris, New York, even in Small Rock—
(NELLIE *looks puzzled*) Where you come from . . .

> (NELLIE *suddenly understands what he means and bursts*
> *out laughing.*)

NELLIE

Oh, Little Rock!

EMILE

(EMILE, *laughing with her and shouting the correction*)
Little Rock! . . . You know fugitives there?

> (NELLIE *runs over to where she has left her bag.*)

NELLIE

I'll show you a picture of a Little Rock fugitive. (*Taking
a clipping from an envelope in the bag*) I got this clipping
from my mother today.

> (*She hands it to* EMILE *who reads:*)

EMILE

"Ensign Nellie Forbush, Arkansas' own Florence Night-
ingale . . ."

NELLIE

(*Apologetically*)

That was written by Mrs. Leeming, the Social Editor. She
went to school with my mother. To read her, you would think
that I'm practically the most important nurse in the entire
Navy and that I run the fleet hospital all by myself, and it's
only a matter of time before I'll be a Lady Admiral.

EMILE

In this picture you do not look much like an Admiral.

NELLIE

Oh, that was taken before I knew what rain and heat and mud could do to your disposition. But it isn't rainy today. Gosh, it's beautiful here. Just look at that yellow sun! You know, I don't think it's the end of the world like everyone else thinks. I can't work myself up to getting that low. (*He smiles*) Do you think I'm crazy too? They all do over at the fleet hospital. You know what they call me? Knucklehead Nellie. I suppose I am, but I can't help it.

(*She sings*)
When the sky is a bright canary yellow
I forget every cloud I've ever seen—
So they call me a cockeyed optimist,
Immature and incurably green!

I have heard people rant and rave and bellow
That we're done and we might as well be dead—
But I'm only a cockeyed optimist
And I can't get it into my head.

I hear the human race
Is falling on its face
And hasn't very far to go,
But every whippoorwill
Is selling me a bill
And telling me it just ain't so!

I could say life is just a bowl of jello
And appear more intelligent and smart
But I'm stuck
(Like a dope!)

8

With a thing called hope,
And I can't get it out of my heart . . . Not this heart!
(She walks over to him, speaking the next line)
Want to know anything else about me?

EMILE

Yes. You say you are a fugitive. When you joined the
Navy, what were you running away from?
(He returns the clipping to her.)

NELLIE

Gosh, I don't know. It was more like running *to* something.
I wanted to see what the world was like—outside Little Rock,
I mean. And I wanted to meet different kinds of people and
find out if I like them better. And I'm finding out.
(She suddenly becomes self-conscious.)

EMILE
(Tactful)
Would you like some cognac?

NELLIE
(Relieved)
I'd love some.
*(EMILE goes to the table and pours the brandy. In the
following verses, EMILE and NELLIE are not singing to
each other. Each is soliloquizing:)*

NELLIE
(Thoughtfully watching EMILE)
Wonder how I'd feel,

9

Living on a hillside,
Looking on an ocean,
Beautiful and still.

EMILE

(Pouring the cognac)

This is what I need,
This is what I've longed for,
Someone young and smiling
Climbing up my hill!

NELLIE

We are not alike;
Probably I'd bore him.
He's a cultured Frenchman—
I'm a little hick.

EMILE

(Pausing as he starts to pour the second glass)

Younger men than I,
Officers and doctors,
Probably pursue her—
She could have her pick.

NELLIE

(She catches his eye. Each averts his eyes from the other)

Wonder why I feel
Jittery and jumpy!
I am like a schoolgirl,
Waiting for a dance.

EMILE

(Carrying the two filled brandy glasses, he approaches NELLIE)*

Can I ask her now?
I am like a schoolboy!

What will be her answer?

Do I have a chance?

(*He passes* NELLIE *her brandy glass. It is a large snifter type of glass. She has apparently never drunk from one before. She watches him carefully as he lifts his to his lips, and does the same. As they drink, the music rises to great ecstatic heights. One is made aware that in this simple act of two people who are falling in love, each drinking brandy, there are turbulent thoughts and feelings going on in their hearts and brains. They lower their glasses. The music dies down.* EMILE *struggles to say something. He plunges into the middle of his subject as if continuing a thought which he assumes she has sensed.*)

EMILE

In peacetime, the boat from America comes once a month. The ladies—the wives of the planters—often go to Australia during the hot months. It can get very hot here.

NELLIE

It can get hot in Arkansas, too.

(*She takes another quick swallow after this one.*)

EMILE

Ah, yes?

NELLIE

(*Nodding her head*)

Uh-huh.

EMILE

(*He puts his glass down on the table*)

I have many books here . . . Marcel Proust? (*She looks*

blank) Anatole France? (*This evokes a faint smile of half-recognition from her*) Did you study French in school?

NELLIE

Oh, yes.

EMILE

Ah, then you can read French?

NELLIE

(*As though saying, "Of course not"*)

No! (*Fearful of having disappointed him, she makes a feeble attempt to add a note of hope*) I can conjugate a few verbs. (*Realizing how silly this must sound to him, she changes the subject*) I bet you read a lot.

EMILE

Out here, one becomes hungry to learn everything. (*He rises and paces nervously*) Not to miss anything, not to let anything good pass by.

(*He pauses and looks down at her, unable to go on. She, feeling he is coming closer to his point, looks up with a sudden encouraging smile.*)

NELLIE

Yes?

EMILE

One waits so long for what is good . . . and when at last it comes, one cannot risk to lose. (*He turns away, searching for more words*) So . . . so one must speak and act quickly even—even if it seems almost foolish to be so quick. (*He looks at her, worried . . . has he gone too far . . . how will she accept any advance at all he may make to her? She can only smile helplessly back at him. He goes on, speaking quickly*) I know it is only two weeks. A dinner given at your Officers' Club. Do you remember?

NELLIE

Yes.

EMILE

That is the way things happen sometimes. . . . Isn't it, Nellie?

NELLIE

(*Swallowing hard*)

Yes, it is . . . Emile.

EMILE

(*Singing*)

Some enchanted evening
You may see a stranger,
You may see a stranger
Across a crowded room—
And somehow you know
(You know even then)
That somewhere you'll see her again and again.

Some enchanted evening
Someone may be laughing,
You may hear her laughing
Across a crowded room—
And night after night
(As strange as it seems)
The sound of her laughter will sing in your dreams.

13

Who can explain it?
Who can tell you why?
Fools give you reasons—
Wise men never try.

Some enchanted evening
When you find your true love,
When you feel her call you
Across a crowded room—
Then fly to her side,
And make her your own,
Or all through your life you may dream all alone. . . .

Once you have found her
Never let her go,
Once you have found her
Never let her go!
(*There follow several seconds of silence. Neither moves.*
EMILE *speaks*)

I am older than you. If we have children, when I die they
will be growing up. You could afford to take them back to
America—if you like. Think about it.
(HENRY *enters.*)

HENRY

Monsieur de Becque, la jeep de Mademoiselle est ici. (NELLIE
and EMILE *turn as if awakened from a dream*) La jeep de
Mademoiselle. (HENRY *smiles, a wide toothy smile, at* NELLIE)
Votre jeep!

NELLIE

Oh, my jeep! (*She looks at her watch*) Gosh! Thank you,
Henry. I'm on duty in ten minutes!
(HENRY *exits.* NELLIE *holds out her hand to* EMILE.)

EMILE

Before you leave, Nellie, I want to tell you something. A while ago, you asked me a question—why did I leave France?

NELLIE

Oh, Emile, that was none of my business.

EMILE

But I want to tell you. I had to leave France. I killed a man.
(*Pause.*)

NELLIE

Why did you kill him?

EMILE

He was a wicked man, a bully. Everyone in our village was glad to see him die, and it was not to my discredit. Do you believe me, Nellie?
(*Another pause—unbearable to him.*)

NELLIE

You have just told me that you killed a man and that it's all right. I hardly know you, and yet I know it's all right.

EMILE

(*Deeply moved*)
Thank you, Nellie. (*His voice suddenly gay and exultant*) And you like my place?

NELLIE

Yes.

EMILE

You will think?

NELLIE

(*Smiling up at him*)

I will think.

(*They are silent and motionless for a moment. Then she turns suddenly and walks off very quickly. He looks after her and starts to hum softly. He picks up the coffee cup she has left on the fountain and smiles down at it. He holds the cup up so he can examine its rim.*)

EMILE

Lipstick! . . . Three lumps of sugar in this little cup! (*He laughs aloud, then resumes his humming and walks, almost dances, across the stage in time to his own music.* NGANA *and* JEROME *enter and walk behind him across the stage, imitating his happy stride. As* EMILE *puts down the cup, the children join him, humming the same melody. He turns quickly and frowns down on them with mock sternness. They giggle*) Eh bien!

JEROME

Bravo, Papa!

(*The children both applaud.*)

EMILE

Merci, Monsieur!

NGANA

Nous chantons bien, aussi.

EMILE

Ah, oui?

NGANA

Attends, Papa!

JEROME
(*Parroting* NGANA)

Attends, Papa!
(*He looks at* NGANA *for the signal to start the song.*
They sing . . . EMILE *conducting them.*)

NGANA AND JEROME

Dites moi
Pourquoi
La vie est belle—
(EMILE *joins them*)
Dites moi
Pourquoi
La vie est gai!
Dites moi
Pourquoi,
(EMILE *and* JEROME *make a deep bow to* NGANA)
Chère Mad'moiselle,
(EMILE *picks them up, one under each arm, and starts*
to carry them off as they finish singing the refrain
together)
Est-ce que
Parce que
Vous m'aimez?
(*The lights fade out and a transparent curtain closes*
in on them. Before they are out of sight, the characters
of the next scene have entered downstage in front of the
curtain. All transitions from one scene to another in the
play are achieved in this manner so that the effect is of
one picture dissolving into the next.)

ACT ONE

Scene II

The curtain depicts no specific place but represents the abstract pattern of a large tapa-cloth. In front of this, lounge a group of Seabees, sailors and Marines. As the lights come up on them and go out on the previous scene, they are singing.

MEN

Bloody Mary is the girl I love,
Bloody Mary is the girl I love,
Bloody Mary is the girl I love—
Now ain't that too damn bad!
Her skin is as tender as DiMaggio's glove,
Her skin is as tender as DiMaggio's glove,
Her skin is as tender as DiMaggio's glove—
Now ain't that too damn bad!

> (*The object of this serenade who has been hidden during the song, by two sailors, is now revealed as they move away. This is* BLOODY MARY. *She is small, yellow, with Oriental eyes. She wears black sateen trousers, and a white blouse over which is an old Marine's tunic. On her head is a peach-basket hat. Around her neck is a G.I. identification chain from which hangs a silver Marine emblem. At the end of the singing, she gives out a shrill cackle of laughter with which we shall soon learn to identify her.*)

MARY

(Looking straight out at the audience)

Hallo, G.I.! *(She holds up a grass skirt)* Grass skirt? Very saxy! Fo' dolla'? Saxy grass skirt. Fo' dolla'! Send home Chicago. You like? You buy? *(Her eyes scan the audience as if following a passer-by. Her crafty smile fades to a quick scowl as he apparently passes without buying. She calls after him)* Where you go? Come back! Chipskate! Crummy G.I.! Sadsack. Droopy-drawers!

MARINE

Tell 'em good, Mary!

MARY

What is good?

MARINE

Tell him he's a stingy bastard!

MARY

(Delighted at the sound of these new words)

Stingy bastard! *(She turns back toward the* MARINE *for approval)* That good?

MARINE

That's great, Mary! You're learning fast.

MARY

(Calling off again)

Stingy bastard! *(She cackles gaily and turns back to the* MARINE*)* I learn fast. . . . Pretty soon I talk English good as any crummy Marine. *(Calling off once more)* Stingy bastard!

(She laughs very loud but the Marines, Seabees and

sailors laugh louder and cheer her. They then resume their serenade.)

MEN

Bloody Mary's chewing betel nuts,
She is always chewing betel nuts,
Bloody Mary's chewing betel nuts—
And she don't use Pepsodent.
(*She grins and shows her betel-stained teeth*)
Now ain't that too damn bad!
(*While this is being sung, the lights come up behind the tapa-cloth transparent curtain revealing:*)

ACT ONE

Scene III

Scene: *The edge of a palm grove near the beach. Beyond the beach in the bay can be seen the same twin-peaked island that was evident from* EMILE'S *hillside. On your left, as you look at the stage, is* BLOODY MARY'S *kiosk. This is made of bamboo and canvas. Her merchandise, laid out in front, comprises shells, native hats, local dress material, outrigger canoes and hookahs. Several grass skirts are hanging up around the kiosk. On the right, at first making a puzzling silhouette, then as the lights come up, resolving itself into a contraption of weird detail, is a G.I. homemade washing machine. It looks partly like a giant ice-cream freezer, partly like a windmill. In front of it there is a sign which reads:*

TWISTED AIR HAND LAUNDRY

LUTHER BILLIS ENTERPRISES

SPECIAL RATES FOR SEABEES

As the lights come up, the washing machine is being operated by Carpenter's Mate, Second Class, George Watts, better known as "STEWPOT." *Seabees, sailors, Marines and some Army men lounge around the scene waiting for whatever diversion* BLOODY MARY *may provide. During the singing which covers this change,* BLOODY MARY *takes a strange-looking object out of her pocket and dangles it in front of a* MARINE.

21

MARINE

What is that thing?

MARY

(*Holding the small object in her hand*)
Is head. Fifty dolla'.

MARINE

(*Revolted*)
What's it *made* of?

MARY

Made outa head! Is real human.

MARINE

(*Fascinated*)
What makes it so small?

MARY

Shlunk! Only way to keep human head is shlink 'em.

MARINE

No, thanks.
(*He leaves quickly.*)

MARY

(*To a new customer as she holds a grass skirt up to her
waist and starts to dance*)
Fo' dolla'. Send home Chicago to saxy sweetheart! She
make wave like this.

(*She starts to dance. One of the sailors grabs her and
goes into an impromptu jitterbug dance with her.
Others join, and soon the beach is alive with gyrating*)

*gentlemen of the United States Armed Services. As this
spontaneous festivity is at its height,* LUTHER BILLIS
enters, followed by the PROFESSOR, *both loaded with
grass skirts. They come down in front of* BLOODY MARY
and throw the grass skirts at her feet.)

BILLIS

Here you are, Sweaty Pie! Put them down, Professor. These
beautiful skirts were made by myself, the Professor here, and
three other Seabees in half the time it takes your native work-
ers to make 'em. (*He picks up a skirt and demonstrates*) See?
No stretch! (*Throwing the skirt back on the ground*) Look
'em over, Sweaty Pie, and give me your price.

(*At this point, an altercation starts upstage near the
washing machine.*)

SAILOR

Look at that shirt!

STEWPOT

Take it up with the manager.
(*He points down to* BILLIS.)

SAILOR
(*Coming down to him*)
Hey, Big Dealer! Hey, Luther Billis!

BILLIS
(*Smoothly*)
What can I do for you, my boy? What's the trouble?

23

SAILOR

(Holding up his shirt which has been laundered and is in tatters)

Look at that shirt!

BILLIS

The Billis Laundry is not responsible for minor burns and tears. *(He turns back laconically to* MARY*)* What do you say, Sweatso? What am I offered?

(The SAILOR *storms off. The* PROFESSOR, *meanwhile, is showing the beautiful work they do to some other sailors and Seabees.)*

PROFESSOR

(Holding up a skirt)

All hand sewn!

SAILOR

Gee, that's mighty nice work!

BILLIS

(To BLOODY MARY*)*

Do you hear that, Sweaty Pie? You can probably sell these to the chumps for five or six dollars apiece. Now, I'll let you have the whole bunch for . . . say . . . eighty bucks.

MARY

Give you ten dolla'.

BILLIS

What?

MARY

Not enough?

BILLIS

You're damn well right, not enough!

MARY

(*Dropping the skirt at his feet*)

Den you damn well keep.

(*She goes down to another sailor and takes from her pocket a boar's tooth bracelet which she holds up to tempt him.*)

BILLIS

(*Following* BLOODY MARY)

Now look here, Dragon Lady— (*Whatever he was about to say is knocked out of his head by the sight of the bracelet.* BILLIS *is an inveterate and passionate souvenir hunter*) What's that you got there, a boar's tooth bracelet? Where'd you get that? (*He points to the twin-peaked island*) Over there on Bali Ha'i?

MARY

(*Smiling craftily*)

You like?

BILLIS

(*Taking bracelet and showing to G.I.'s who have huddled around him*)

You know what that is? A bracelet made out of a single boar's tooth. They cut the tooth from the boar's mouth in a big ceremonial over there on Bali Ha'i. There ain't a souvenir you can pick up in the South Pacific as valuable as this . . . What do you want for it, Mary?

MARY

Hundred dolla'!

BILLIS

Hundred dollars! (*Shocked, but realizing he will pay it, turns to the boys and justifies himself in advance*) That's cheap. I thought it would be more.

(*He takes the money from his pocket.*)

PROFESSOR

I don't see how she can do it.

MARY

Make you special offer Big Deala'. I trade you boar's tooth bracelet for all grass skirts.

BILLIS

It's a deal.

MARY

Wait a minute. Is no deal till you throw in something for good luck.

BILLIS

Okay. What do you want me to throw in?

MARY

(*Taking money from his hand*)
Hundred dolla'.

BILLIS

Well, for the love of . . .

MARY

(*Shaking his hand, grinning a big Oriental grin*)
Good luck.

26

(She exits with grass skirts. The men all crowd around BILLIS, *shaking his hand in ironic "congratulation.")*

BILLIS

You don't run into these things every day. They're scarce as hens' teeth.

PROFESSOR

They're bigger, too.

BILLIS

That damned Bali Ha'i! (*Turning and looking toward the twin-peaked island*) Why does it have to be off limits? You can get everything over there. Shrunken heads, bracelets, old ivory—

SAILOR

Young French women!

BILLIS

Knock off! I'm talking about souvenirs.

PROFESSOR

So's he.

BILLIS

(Pacing restlessly)

We got to get a boat and get over there. I'm feeling held down again. I need to take a trip.

STEWPOT

Only officers can sign out boats.

BILLIS

I'll get a boat all right. I'll latch onto some officer who's

27

got some imagination . . . that would like to see that Boar's Tooth ceremonial as much as I would . . . It's a hell of a ceremonial! Dancin', drinkin' . . . everything!

SAILOR

Why, you big phony. We all know why you want to go to Bali Ha'i.

BILLIS

Why?

SAILOR

Because the French planters put all their young women over there when they heard the G.I.'s were coming. That's why! It ain't boar's teeth . . . it's women!

BILLIS

It is boar's teeth . . . *and* women!
(*A long pause. All the men are still and thoughtful, each dreaming a similar dream—but his own. Music starts. A* SEABEE *breaks the silence.*)

SEABEE
(*Singing*)

We got sunlight on the sand,
We got moonlight on the sea.

SAILOR

We got mangoes and bananas
You can pick right off a tree.

MARINE

We got volley ball and ping pong
And a lot of dandy games—

28

BILLIS

What ain't we got?

ALL

We ain't got dames!

MARINE

We get packages from home,

SAILOR

We get movies, we get shows,

STEWPOT

We get speeches from our skipper

SOLDIER

And advice from Tokyo Rose

SEABEE

We get letters doused wit' poifume,

SAILOR

We get dizzy from the smell—

BILLIS

What don't we get?

ALL

You know damn well!

BILLIS

We have nothin' to put on a clean, white suit for.
What we need is what there ain't no substitute for!

29

ALL

There is nothin' like a dame
Nothin' in the world.
There is nothin' you can name
That is anythin' like a dame.

MARINE

We feel restless,
We feel blue.

SEABEE

We feel lonely and, in brief,
We feel every kind of feelin'

PROFESSOR

But the feelin' of relief.

SAILOR

We feel hungry as the wolf felt
When he met Red Riding Hood—

ALL

What don't we feel?

STEWPOT

We don't feel good!

SAILOR

Lots of things in life are beautiful, but brother—
There is one particular thing that is nothin' whatsoever in
        any way shape or form like any other!

ALL

There is nothin' like a dame—
Nothin' in the world.
There is nothin' you can name
That is anythin' like a dame.

Nothin' else is built the same,
Nothin' in the world
Has a soft and wavy frame
Like the silhouette of a dame.

MARINE
(*With a deep bass voice*)

There is absolutely nothin' like the frame of a dame!
(*The music continues throughout the following dialogue and action.*)

GIRL'S VOICE

Hut, two, three, four! Get—your—exercise!
(*A husky* NURSE *enters, leading several other* NURSES, *all dressed in bathing suits, playsuits, or fatigues.* NELLIE *is among them. They jog across the stage, their* LEADER *continuing the military count. The men's eyes follow them.*)

A TIRED NURSE

Can't we rest a while?

HUSKY LEADER

Come on you nurses, pick it up!
(NELLIE *drops out of line as the others run off.*)

NELLIE
(*Beckoning to* BILLIS)

Hey, Luther!

STEWPOT
(*Nudging* BILLIS)

Luther!

(BILLIS *turns and goes shyly to* NELLIE, *terribly embarrassed that the men are watching him. He is a different* BILLIS *in front of* NELLIE. *He is unassured and has lost all of his brashness. For him,* NELLIE FORBUSH *has "class."*)

BILLIS

Yes, Miss Forbush.
(*All eyes follow him.*)

NELLIE

Have you done what you promised?

BILLIS

Yes, Miss Forbush. (*He pulls out a newspaper package from a hiding place in the roots of a tree and hands it to her*) I did it all last night. (*With an alarmed look at his comrades, as she starts to unwrap it*) You don't have to open it now!

(*But* NELLIE *opens the package, much to* BILLIS' *embarrassment. It is her laundry, neatly folded.*)

NELLIE

Oh. You do beautiful work, Luther! (*Two men painfully cling to each other and turn their heads away.* BILLIS *tries to outglare the others in defensive defiance*) You've even done the pleats in my shorts!

32

BILLIS

Aw, pleats aren't hard. You better run along now and catch up to your gang.

NELLIE

Pleats are *very* hard. How do you do such delicate work at night, in the dark?

BILLIS

There was a moon!

STEWPOT

(*In a syrupy voice*)

There was a moon!

BILLIS

(*He turns to the men, realizing that they have heard this, and shouts defiantly*)

A full moon!

NELLIE

(*She is wrapping up the package*)

How much, Luther!

BILLIS

(*Earnestly*)

Oh, no, not from you.

NELLIE

Gosh, I guess I'm just about the luckiest nurse on this island to have found you. You're a treasure. (*She turns and runs off*) Well, good-bye, Luther. Hut, two, three, four!

(*She has gone!* BILLIS *turns and faces the men, trying to bluff it out. He walks belligerently over to* STEWPOT *who with the* PROFESSOR *whistles "There's Nothin' Like a Dame." Then he walks over to another group and*

33

30241

they join STEWPOT *and* PROFESSOR *in whistling. Soon all are whistling.* BILLIS *whistles too. After the refrain is finished,* STEWPOT *looks off reflectively at the departing* NELLIE.)

STEWPOT

She's a nice little girl, but some of them nurses—the officers can have them.

PROFESSOR

They got them!

STEWPOT

Well, they can have them!

MARINE
(*Singing*)

So suppose a dame ain't bright,
Or completely free from flaws,

SAILOR

Or as faithful as a bird dog,

SEABEE

Or as kind as Santa Claus,

SOLDIER

It's a waste of time to worry
Over things that they have not

SAILOR

Be thankful for

ALL

The things they got!

34

HUSKY LEADER
(Entering)
Hut, two, three, four. Hut, two, three, four!
(The exercising nurses enter upstage, jogging in the opposite direction to their previous course. NELLIE is again with them. She turns and waves to BILLIS and points to the laundry under her arm. The boys all rise and turn upstage, their heads following the girls until they're off. Then the boys continue to turn until they're facing front again.)

ALL
There is nothin' you can name
That is anythin' like a dame!
There are no books like a dame,
And nothin' looks like a dame,
There are no drinks like a dame,
And nothin' thinks like a dame,
Nothin' acts like a dame
Or attracts like a dame.
There ain't a thing that's wrong with any man here
That can't be cured by puttin' him near
A girly, womanly, female, feminine dame!
(BLOODY MARY enters and starts humming the song, as she proceeds to rearrange her new stock of grass skirts. LT. JOSEPH CABLE enters. He wears suntans, overseas cap, and carries a musette bag in his hand. BLOODY MARY sees him and stops singing. They stand for a moment, looking at each other—she, suspicious and frightened, and he, puzzled and curious.)

35

MARY

Hallo.

CABLE

Hello.

(*Music of "Bali Ha'i" is played softly.*)

MARY

You mak' trouble for me?

CABLE

Hunh?

MARY

Are you crummy major?

CABLE

No, I'm even crummier than that. I'm a lieutenant.

MARY

Lootellan?

CABLE

(*Laughing*)

Lootellan.

(*He strolls away from her, toward the men.*)

BILLIS

Hiya, Lootellan. New on the rock?

CABLE

Just came in on that PBY.

BILLIS

Yeah? Where from?

36

CABLE

A little island south of Marie Louise.

STEWPOT

Then you been up where they use real bullets!

CABLE

Unh-huh.

MARY

(*Who has been looking adoringly at* CABLE)
Hey, Lootellan. You damn saxy man!

CABLE

(*Rocked off his balance for a moment*)
Thanks. You're looking pretty—er—fit yourself.
(*She grins happily at him, showing her betel-stained teeth and crosses, beaming, to her assistant.*)

MARY

(*To assistant*)
Damn saxy!

CABLE

(*To* BILLIS)
Who is she?

BILLIS

She's Tonkinese—used to work for a French planter.

MARY

French planters stingy bastards!
(*She laughs.*)

37

CABLE

Say, I wonder if any of you know a French planter named de Becque?

BILLIS

Emile de Becque? I think he's the guy lives on top of that hill . . . Do you know him?

CABLE

(*Looking off toward the hill, thoughtfully*)
No, but I'm going to.
(MARY *follows* CABLE, *taking the shrunken head from her pocket.*)

MARY

Hey, Lootellan! Real human head! . . . You got sweetheart? Send home Chicago to saxy sweetheart!

CABLE

No—er—she's a Philadelphia girl.

MARY

Whazzat, Philadelia girl? Whazzat mean? No saxy? (*With a sudden impulse*) You like I give you free?

BILLIS

Free! You never give *me* anything free.

MARY

You not saxy like Lootellan. (*To* CABLE, *proffering the shrunken head*) Take!

CABLE

No, thanks. Where'd you get that anyway?

MARY

Bali Ha'i.

STEWPOT

(*Nudging* BILLIS, *pointing to* CABLE, *as he whispers:*)
There's your officer! There's your officer!

BILLIS

That's that island over there with the two volcanoes. (*Significantly*) *Officers* can get launches and go over there.

CABLE

(*Looking out at island*)
Bali Ha'i . . . What does that mean?

MARY

Bali Ha'i mean "I am your special Island" . . . mean . . . "Here I am." Bali Ha'i is *your* special Island, Lootellan. I know! You listen! You hear island call to you. Listen! You no hear something? Listen!

CABLE

(*After listening for a moment*)
I hear the sound of the wind and the waves, that's all.

MARY

You no hear something calling? Listen!
(*Silence.* ALL *listen.*)

STEWPOT

(*Trying to be helpful*)
I think *I* hear something.

39

BILLIS

(In a harsh, threatening whisper)
Shut your big fat mouth!

MARY

Hear voice?
   (She sings to CABLE, *as he gazes out at the mysterious
   island)*
Mos' people live on a lonely island,
Lost in de middle of a foggy sea.
Mos' people long fo' anudder island
One where dey know dey would lak to be . . .

   Bali Ha'i
   May call you,
   Any night, any day.
   In your heart
   You'll hear it call you
   "Come away, come away."

   Bali Ha'i
   Will whisper
   On de wind of de sea,
   "Here am I,
   Your special island!
   Come to me, come to me!"

   Your own special hopes,
   Your own special dreams
   Bloom on de hillside
   And shine in de streams.

If you try,
You'll find me
Where de sky meets de sea,
"Here am I,
Your special island!
Come to me, come to me!"

Bali Ha'i!
  Bali Ha'i!
    Bali Ha'i!

Some day, you'll see me,
Floatin' in de sunshine,
My head stickin' out
F'um a low-flyin' cloud.
You'll hear me call you,
Singin' through de sunshine,
Sweet and clear as can be,
"Come to me,
Here am I,
Come to me!"

If you try,
You'll find me
Where de sky meets de sea,
"Here am I,
Your special island!
Come to me, come to me!"

Bali Ha'i!
  Bali Ha'i!
    Bali Ha'i!

(BLOODY MARY *exits.* CABLE *seems spellbound by her words.* BILLIS *follows up with a more earthy form of salesmanship.*)

BILLIS

Of course, Lieutenant, right now that island is off limits due to the fact that the French planters have all their young women running around over there. (*He pauses to observe the effect of these significant words*) Of course, you being an officer, you could get a launch. I'd even be willing to requisition a boat for you. What do you say, Lieutenant?

(*Singing throatily*)
Bali Ha'i may call you
Any night any day.
In your heart you'll
Hear it call you—
Bali Ha'i—Bali Ha'i . . .
Hunh, Lieutenant?
　　(*Pause.*)

CABLE

No.

BILLIS

(*Making a quick shift*)

I see what you mean, being off limits and all. It would take a lot of persuading to get *me* to go over there . . . But, another thing goes on over there—the ceremonial of the boar's tooth. After they kill the boar they pass around some of that coconut liquor and women dance with just skirts on . . . (*His voice becoming evil*) and everybody gets to know everybody pretty well . . .
　　(*He sings*)

Bali Ha'i will whisper—
> (BILLIS *starts dance as he hums the melody seductively.*
> *Then he stops and talks*)

It's just a little tribal ceremonial and I thought you being up in the shooting war for such a long time without getting any—recreation—I thought you might be interested.

CABLE

I am. But right now I've got to report to the Island Commander.

BILLIS

Oh. (*Shouting officiously*) Professor! Take the Lieutenant up in the truck.

CABLE

Professor?

BILLIS

That's because he went to college. You go to college?

CABLE

Er—yes.

BILLIS

Where?

CABLE

A place in New Jersey.

BILLIS

Where? Rutgers?

CABLE

No . . . Princeton.

BILLIS

Oh. Folks got money, eh, Lieutenant? (*He leers wisely*)

43

Don't be ashamed of it. We understand. Say! Maybe you'd like to hear the Professor talk some language. What would you like to hear? Latin? Grecian? (*Grabbing the unwilling* PROFESSOR *by the arm and leading him over to* CABLE) Aw, give him some Latin!

PROFESSOR

(*The* PROFESSOR *feels pretty silly, but proceeds:*)
"Rectius vives Licini—"

BILLIS

Ain't that beautiful!

PROFESSOR

". . . neque altum
Semper urgendo dum procellas . . ."
(*A crowd gathers around the* PROFESSOR. BILLIS *beams at* CABLE.)

BILLIS

Now, Lieutenant, what did he say?

CABLE

I'm afraid I haven't the slightest idea.

BILLIS

What's the matter, didn't you graduate? (*Disgusted, to the* PROFESSOR) Take the Lieutenant to the buildings.
(CABLE *and the* PROFESSOR *start to go.*)

PROFESSOR

Aye, aye!

BILLIS

(*To* STEWPOT)
He'll never make Captain.

44

(*The* PROFESSOR, *suddenly alarmed by something he sees offstage, turns back and starts to make strange signal-noises of warning.*)

PROFESSOR

Whoop-whoop-whoop! (*In a hoarse whisper*) Iron Belly! (*The men assume casual and innocent attitudes. Some make bird sounds.* MARY *looks off and walks back to her kiosk to stand defiantly in front of it.* CABLE, *puzzled, stands by to await developments. What develops is that "Iron Belly,"* CAPTAIN BRACKETT, *enters, followed by his executive officer,* COMMANDER HARBISON.)

HARBISON
(*A brusque man*)

Here she is, sir.
(*He points to* BLOODY MARY, *who is standing her ground doggedly in front of her kiosk.* BRACKETT *walks slowly over to her.* HARBISON *takes a few steps toward the men and they move away.* BRACKETT *glares at* MARY. *Undaunted, she glares right back.*)

BRACKETT

You are causing an economic revolution on this island. These French planters can't find a native to pick a coconut or milk a cow because you're paying them ten times as much to make these ridiculous grass skirts.

MARY

French planters stingy bastards!
(STEWPOT *drops a tin bucket. The men control them-*

selves by great efforts, their faces contorted queerly.
BRACKETT *scowls and for the moment can think of no
answer.* BILLIS *approaches him, with a snappy salute.*)

BILLIS

Sir! May I make a suggestion, sir?

BRACKETT
(*Returning salute*)

Who are you?

BILLIS

Billis, sir, Luther Billis. (*Making an impressive announce-
ment*) The natives can now go back to work on the farms.
The demand for grass skirts can now be met by us Seabees!

BRACKETT

Dressmakers! (*Starting to blow up*) Do you mean to tell
me the Seabees of the United States Navy are now a lot of—

BILLIS

If you don't like the idea, sir, we can drop it right here, sir.
Just say the word. Just pretend I never brought it up.

HARBISON
(*Reflectively*)

Luther Billis.

BILLIS

Yes, sir?

HARBISON

Nothing. Just making a mental note. I want to be sure
not to forget your name.

46

(*Pause, during which* BILLIS *slowly and dejectedly retires.* BRACKETT *turns to* MARY.)

BRACKETT

I want to see you pick up every scrap of this paraphernalia now! And, for the last time, carry it way down there beyond that fence off Navy property.

(MARY *stands firmly planted and immovable!* . . . CABLE *walks to the kiosk and collapses it.*)

CABLE
(*With decisive authority*)

Come on, everybody. Take all this stuff and throw it over that fence.

(*The men quickly obey,* BILLIS *ostentatiously taking charge in front of the two officers.*)

BILLIS
(*To men*)

All right—take it way down there. Off Navy property!

CABLE
(*Strides over to* MARY *and points off*)

You go too!

MARY
(CABLE *can do no wrong in her eyes*)

All right, Lootellan. Thank you.

(*She exits. By this time, all the men have gone, taking her kiosk with them.* BRACKETT, CABLE *and* HARBISON *are left.* BRACKETT *looks at* HARBISON *as if to ask who* CABLE *is.* HARBISON *shrugs his shoulders.* CABLE *turns and exchanges salutes with* BRACKETT.)

47

BRACKETT

Lieutenant, who are you, anyway?

CABLE

I'm Lieutenant Joseph Cable, sir. I just flew in on that PBY.

BRACKETT

A joy ride?

CABLE

No, sir. Orders.

BRACKETT

A Marine under orders to me?

CABLE

Yes, sir.

BRACKETT

I'm Captain Brackett.

CABLE

How do you do, sir?

BRACKETT

This is Commander Harbison, my Executive Officer. (CABLE *and* HARBISON *exchange hellos, salutes and handshakes*) Well, what's it all about?

CABLE

My Colonel feels that all these islands are in danger because none of us has been getting first-hand intelligence, and what we need is a coast watch.

HARBISON

A coast watch?

CABLE

A man with a radio hiding out on one of those Jap-held islands, where he could watch for Jap ships when they start down the bottleneck . . . down this way.

BRACKETT

(*Turning to* HARBISON)

What do you think, Bill?

HARBISON

Well, sir, our pilots could do a hell of a lot to Jap convoys with information like that.

BRACKETT

You'd have to sneak this man ashore at night from a submarine.

CABLE

Yes, sir.

HARBISON

Who's going to do it?

CABLE

Well, sir . . . *I've* been elected.

(*Pause.*)

BRACKETT

(*After exchanging a look with* HARBISON)

You've got quite an assignment, son.

HARBISON

How long do you think you could last there, sending out messages, before the Japs found you?

49

CABLE

I think I'd be okay if I could take a man with me who really knew the country. Headquarters has found out there's a French civilian here who used to have a plantation on Marie Louise Island.

HARBISON

Marie Louise! That's a good spot. Right on the bottleneck.

BRACKETT

What's this Frenchman's name?

CABLE

Emile de Becque.

BRACKETT
(*Suddenly excited*)
Meet me in my office in about half an hour, Cable.
(*He starts off, followed by* HARBISON.)

CABLE

Yes, sir.

BRACKETT

Come on, Bill! Maybe we'll get in this war yet!
(*They exit.* CABLE *watches them off, then picks up his musette bag and starts off himself. The music of "Bali Ha'i" is played.* CABLE *stops in his tracks and listens. Then he turns and looks across at the island. . . . Softly, he starts to sing:*)

CABLE

Bali Ha'i may call you
Any night,

Any day,
In your heart you'll hear it call you,
Come away, come away.
Bali Ha'i, Bali Ha'i, Bali Ha'i.

ACT ONE

Scene IV

As CABLE *sings, the lights fade slowly. A transparent curtain closes across him.*

Downstage, several G.I.'s enter carrying bales and various articles of equipment. The lights dim out on CABLE *behind the curtain and now, illuminating the forestage, reveal the curtain as depicting a company street.*

SAILOR

(Crossing stage)

When are you guys going to get that lumber down in our area?

SEABEE

(Passing him)

Aw, knock it off!

SAILOR

We'll never get it finished by Thanksgiving.

(By this time, the lights are higher on the company street. Natives and G.I.'s are constantly crossing, carrying equipment. Natives are seen sometimes wearing G.I. uniforms and sometimes just native cloths. Two nurses in white uniforms cross. Then BILLIS *enters, in earnest conversation with* STEWPOT *and the* PROFESSOR.)

52

BILLIS

Did you tell those guys at the shop to stop making those grass skirts?

STEWPOT

Sure, they just turned out one of these. (*He hands him a small, dark object*) What do you think of it?

BILLIS
(*Studying it a moment*)
That don't look like a dried-up human head. It looks like an old orange painted with shoe-polish.

STEWPOT

That's what it is.

BILLIS

Go back to the shop and tell them to try again. If I order a dried-up human head, I want a human head . . . dried up!
(*He puts the orange in his pocket.*)

STEWPOT

But—

BILLIS

Fade. Here he comes. (STEWPOT *and the* PROFESSOR *move away as* CABLE *enters.* BILLIS *crosses to him and speaks to him in a low voice, right in* CABLE's *ear, as he walks alongside him*) Don't change your expression, Lieutenant. Just act like we're talking casual. I got the boat.

CABLE
(Stops)

What boat?

BILLIS

Keep walking down the company street. Keep your voice down. (CABLE *walks slowly and uncertainly*) I signed out a boat in your name. We're shoving off for Bali Ha'i in forty-five minutes.

CABLE
(Stopping)
No, we're not. I've got to see Captain Brackett.

BILLIS
(An injured man)
Lieutenant! What are you doing to me? I signed this boat out in your name.

CABLE

Then you're just the man to go back and cancel it. (*Very firmly*) Forget the whole thing. Okay?
(CABLE *walks off.* BILLIS *looks after him with narrowing eyes and jaw thrust forward.*)

BILLIS

Lieutenant, you and me are going on a boat trip whether you like it or not.
(*He pulls the orange, covered with shoe polish, out of his pocket, and wishing to vent his rage somehow, he turns and hurls it off in the direction opposite that taken by* CABLE.)

54

A FURIOUS VOICE
(*Offstage*)

Hey! Who the hell threw that?

BILLIS

(*Spoiling for a fight with anyone at all*)

I threw it! What are you gonna do about it?

(*He strides off pugnaciously in the direction of the voice. Before he is off, the curtains have parted on the succeeding scene.*)

ACT ONE

Scene V

Inside the Island Commander's office. BRACKETT *is sitting at his desk, reading some papers.* HARBISON *stands above him.* CABLE *sits on a chair facing the desk.*

BRACKETT
(*As curtains part*)
Cable . . . we've got some dope on your Frenchman. (*He reads a paper before him*) Marie Louise Island . . . moved down here sixteen years ago . . . lived with a Polynesian woman for about five years . . . two children by her. She died . . . Here's one thing we've got to clear up. Seems he left France in a hurry. Killed a guy. What do you think of that?

CABLE
Might be a handy man to have around.
(*The phone rings.*)

HARBISON
(*Beckoning to* CABLE)
Cable.
(CABLE *joins him and they inspect a map on the wall.*)

BRACKETT
(*In phone*)
Good . . . send her in. No, we haven't got time for her to

56

change into her uniform. Tell her to come in. (*The men exchange looks and face the doorway where presently* NELLIE *appears*) Come in, Miss Forbush.

NELLIE

Captain Brackett, please excuse the way . . .

BRACKETT

You look fine. May I present Commander Harbison?

HARBISON

I have the pleasure of meeting Miss Forbush twice a week. (BRACKETT *looks at him, surprised and curious*) We serve together on the G.I. Entertainment Committee.

BRACKETT

Oh. May I also present Lt. Joseph Cable . . . Miss Forbush. Sit down, Miss Forbush. (*The three men rush to help her sit.* CABLE *gets there first.* NELLIE *sits.* BRACKETT *sits on his desk facing her.* CABLE *drops upstage.* BRACKETT *starts off with light conversation*) How's the Thanksgiving Entertainment coming along?

NELLIE

Very well, thank you, sir. We practice whenever we get a chance.

(*She wonders why she has been sent for.*)

BRACKETT

About a week ago, you had lunch with a French planter . . . Emile de Becque.

57

NELLIE

Yes, sir.

BRACKETT

What do you know about him?

NELLIE

(*Thrown off balance*)

Well, I er . . . what do I know about him?

BRACKETT

That's right.

NELLIE

I . . . we . . . met at the Officers' Club dance. He was there and I . . . met him. (*She stops, hoping they will help her along, but they say nothing, so she has to continue*) Then I had lunch with him that day. . . .

BRACKETT

(*Quickly*)

Yes! Now, what kind of a man is he?

NELLIE

He's very nice . . . He's kind . . . He's attractive. I—er—I just don't know what you want to know, sir.

HARBISON

Miss Forbush, Captain Brackett wants to know, did you discuss politics?

NELLIE

No, sir.

58

BRACKETT

(*After a long, pitying look at* HARBISON)
Would you have discussed politics, Commander? (*Turning back to* NELLIE) Now, what we are specifically interested in is—er—when these fellows come out from France, it's generally because they've had some trouble. (NELLIE *looks worried*) Now . . . has he ever told you anything about that? (NELLIE *hesitates a moment, deliberating just how far to go in her answer.* BRACKETT *tries to help her out, sensing her embarrassment*) What do you know about his family?

NELLIE

(*Glad to be able to answer a simple specific question without incriminating* EMILE)
He has no family—no wife, nobody.

HARBISON

He hasn't any children?
(CABLE *and* HARBISON *exchange looks.*)

NELLIE

No, sir!

BRACKETT

And you say he's never told you why he left France?
(*Pause. Then* NELLIE *answers as a Navy Ensign should.*)

NELLIE

Yes, sir. He left France because he killed a man.
(*A sigh of relief from* BRACKETT.)

59

HARBISON

Did he tell you why?

NELLIE

No. But he will if I ask him.

HARBISON

Well, Miss Forbush, that's exactly what we'd like to have you do. Find out as much as you can about him, his background, his opinions, and why he killed this man in France.

NELLIE

In other words, you want me to spy on him.

BRACKETT

Well, I'm afraid it *is* something like that.

NELLIE

Why? (*Alarmed, she rises and faces* BRACKETT *across his desk*) Do you suspect him of anything?

BRACKETT

(*Lies do not come easy to him*)

No, it's just that we don't know very much about him and he's—er . . . Will you help us, Miss Forbush?
(*Pause.*)

NELLIE

I'll try.

BRACKETT

Thank you. You may go now if you wish.

60

(*She starts toward the door, then turns, thoughtfully, as if asking the question of herself.*)

NELLIE

I don't know very much about him really—do I?
(*Slowly, she goes out. For a moment, the men are silent.*)

CABLE

He's kept a few secrets from her, hasn't he?

BRACKETT

Well, you don't spring a couple of Polynesian kids on a woman right off the bat!

HARBISON

I'm afraid we aren't going to get much out of her. She's obviously in love with him.

CABLE

(*To* HARBISON)
That's hard to believe, sir. They tell me he's a middle-aged man.

BRACKETT

(*Rising from his desk chair. Smoldering*)
Cable! It is a common mistake for boys of your age and athletic ability to underestimate men who have reached their maturity.

CABLE

I didn't mean, sir . . .

61

BRACKETT

Young women frequently find a grown man attractive, strange as it may seem to you. I myself am over fifty. I am a bachelor and, Cable, I do not, by any means, consider myself— through. (*To* HARBISON *who is suppressing laughter*) What's the matter, Bill?

HARBISON

Nothing, evidently!

BRACKETT

O.K., Cable. See you at chow. Do you play bridge?

CABLE

Yes, sir.

BRACKETT

Got any money?

CABLE

Yes, sir.

BRACKETT

I'll take it away from you.

CABLE

Yes, sir.

(*He goes out.* BRACKETT *darts a penetrating look at* HARBISON.)

BRACKETT

What makes you so *damn sure* this mission won't work out?

HARBISON

(*Looking at the map*)

Marie Louise Island is twenty-four miles long and three

62

miles wide. Let's say that every time they send out a message they move to another hill. It seems to me, looking at this thing—

BRACKETT

Realistically.

HARBISON

. . . realistically, (*Measuring his words*) they could last about a week.

(*Pause.* BRACKETT *considers this.*)

BRACKETT

Of course, it would be worth it, if it were the right week. With decent information, our side might get moving. Operation Alligator might get off its can.

YEOMAN

(*Entering with large cardboard box*)

Here it is, sir, I got it.

BRACKETT

(*To* HARBISON)

Okay, Bill. See you at chow. (HARBISON *looks at the package curiously*) *See you at chow, Bill.*

HARBISON

(*Snapping out of it*)

Oh, see you at chow.

(*He goes out.*)

BRACKETT

Got the address right?

YEOMAN

I think so, sir. (*Reading the box lid*) Mrs. Amelia Fortuna. Three twenty-five Euclid Avenue, Shaker Heights, Cleveland, Ohio.

BRACKETT

That's right. I want to pack it myself.

YEOMAN

Yes, sir.

(YEOMAN *exits.* BRACKETT *starts to whistle. He opens the package and takes out a bright yellow grass skirt and shakes it out.* HARBISON *re-enters, stands in doorway, unseen by* BRACKETT, *nods as if his suspicions were confirmed and exits as the lights fade.*)

ACT ONE

Scene VI

As the lights are fading on the Captain's hut, the company-street curtain closes in and the activity seen here before is resumed.

G.I.'s and natives cross, carrying various items of equipment.

NELLIE *enters, walking slowly as she reads a letter. Another* NURSE *in working uniform has some letters in her hand and is moving off.*

NURSE

Going back to the beach, Nellie?

> (NELLIE *nods.* NURSE *exits.* CABLE *enters and watches* NELLIE *for a moment.* NELLIE *is now standing still, reading a part of her letter that evokes an occasional groan of irritation from her.* CABLE *grins at her.*)

CABLE

Letter from home?

> (NELLIE *looks up, startled by his voice, then grins back at him.*)

NELLIE

Yes. Do you get letters from your mother, telling you that everything you do is wrong?

CABLE

No. My mother thinks everything I do is right. . . . Of course, I don't tell her everything I do.

NELLIE

My mother's so prejudiced.

CABLE

Against Frenchmen?
(*She smiles to acknowledge that she gets the allusion, then pursues her anti-maternal tirade.*)

NELLIE

Against anyone outside of Little Rock. She makes a big thing out of two people having different backgrounds.

CABLE

(*Rather hopefully*)

Ages?

NELLIE

Oh, no. Mother says older men are better for girls than younger men.

CABLE

(*Remembering his recent lecture from* BRACKETT *on this subject*)

This has been a discouraging day for me.

NELLIE

Do you agree with Mother about people having things in common? For instance, if the man likes symphony music and the girl likes Dinah Shore—and he reads Marcel Proust and she doesn't read anything . . . Well, what do *you* think? Do you think Mother's right?

66

CABLE

Well, she might be.

NELLIE

Well, I don't think she is.

CABLE

Well, maybe she's not.

NELLIE

Well, good-bye, Lieutenant. You've helped a lot.

CABLE

Listen, you don't know so much about that guy. You better read that letter over two or three times . . .

NELLIE

I'll show you what I think of that idea.
(*She crumples the letter and throws it on the ground.*)

CABLE

Well, don't say I didn't warn you.
(*He exits.* NELLIE *comes back and picks up the letter and starts reading as she walks off.*)

ACT ONE

Scene VII

Before NELLIE *is off the lights come up on:*
The beach. Several nurses are lounging about before taking
their swim. More enter. One of them, DINAH, *is washing an*
evening dress in a tin tub. Upstage is a home-made shower
bath, bearing a sign:

BILLIS BATH CLUB

SHOWER 15¢

USE OF SOAP 5¢

NO TOWELS SUPPLIED

Two or three SEABEES *stand in attendance, part of* BILLIS'
business empire, no doubt.

BILLIS
(Entering)
Oh, I thought Miss Forbush was here. I brought some hot
water for her. (*He goes to shower, climbs a ladder and pours
a bucket of water into the tank on top*) She likes to take a
shampoo Fridays.

NELLIE
(Entering)
Hello, Luther.

BILLIS
Hello, Miss Forbush. I brought some hot water for you.

68

NELLIE

Thanks. It'll do me a lot of good to get some of this sand out of my hair.

BILLIS

If you need some extra water for rinsing your hair, my bath-club concession boys will take care of you. When you're ready for the shower, just pull this chain, just like you was . . . Like you was pulling down a window shade. Take care of her, boys.

(*He exits.* NELLIE *enters the shower.*)

NURSE

What'd he want?

NELLIE

Huh?

NURSE

What'd he want?

NELLIE

Who?

NURSE

Iron Belly.

NELLIE

Captain Brackett? Oh, nothing—nothing important. Something about the Thanksgiving show.

SECOND NURSE

Then what's the trouble, Knucklehead?

NELLIE

Huh?

(*She is now soaking her hair and it is difficult for her to hear.*)

SECOND NURSE

I said, what's the trouble?

NELLIE

Oh, nothing. (*The girls look at one another.* NELLIE *comes out of the shower enclosure*) There's not going to be any trouble any more because I've made up my mind about one thing. (*She takes a deep breath and looks at them dramatically*) It's all off.

(*She goes back into the shower enclosure.*)

THIRD NURSE

With him?

NELLIE

(*Coming right out again through the swinging doors*) Unh-hunh. (*She starts back, then stops and turns*) I'm going to break it off clean before it's too late.

FOURTH NURSE

Knucklehead, what's happened? What'd he do?

NELLIE

He didn't do anything. It's just that . . . Well, I guess I don't know anything about him really and before I go any further with this thing—I just better not get started! Don't you think so, too? Diney?

DINAH

Yes, I do.

NELLIE

(*Unprepared for such prompt and unequivocal agreement*)
You do? Well, I guess I do, too. (*She turns to the other girls*) Well, don't look so dramatic about it. Things like this happen every day.

(*She sings:*)
I'm gonna wash that man right outa my hair,
I'm gonna wash that man right outa my hair,
I'm gonna wash that man right outa my hair,
And send him on his way!

(*She struts around splashing soap out of her hair*)
Get the picture?

I'm gonna wave that man right outa my arms,
I'm gonna wave that man right outa my arms,
I'm gonna wave that man right outa my arms,
And send him on his way!

Don't try to patch it up—

NURSES

Tear it up, tear it up!

NELLIE

Wash him out, dry him out—

NURSES

Push him out, fly him out!

NELLIE

Cancel him and let him go—

71

NURSES

Yea, sister!

I'm gonna wash that man right outa my hair,
I'm gonna wash that man right outa my hair,
I'm gonna wash that man right outa my hair,
And send him on his way!

NELLIE

If the man don't understand you,
If you fly on separate beams,
Waste no time!
Make a change,
Ride that man right off your range,
Rub him outa the roll call
And drum him outa your dreams!

NURSES

Oh-ho!

DINAH

If you laugh at different comics,

ANOTHER NURSE

If you root for different teams,

NELLIE, DINAH, SECOND NURSE

Waste no time,
Weep no more,
Show him what the door is for!

72

NURSES

Rub him outa the roll call
And drum him outa your dreams!

NELLIE

You can't light a fire when the wood's all wet,

GIRLS

No!

NELLIE

You can't make a butterfly strong,

GIRLS

Uh-uh!

NELLIE

You can't fix an egg when it ain't quite good,

NURSES

And you can't fix a man when he's wrong!

NELLIE

You can't put back a petal when it falls from a flower,
Or sweeten up a feller when he starts turning sour—
(NELLIE *goes back into the shower, turns on the water
and rinses the soap out of her hair.*)

NURSES

Oh no, Oh no!
If his eyes get dull and fishy
When you look for glints and gleams,
Waste no time,

Make a switch,
Drop him in the nearest ditch!
Rub him outa the roll call
And drum him outa your dreams!
Oh-ho! Oh-ho!

NELLIE

(*Poking her head out from the shower, then dancing down to the nurses, as she sings:*)
I went and washed that man right outa my hair,
I went and washed that man right outa my hair,
I went and washed that man right outa my hair,
And sent him on his way!

NURSES

She went and washed that man right outa her hair,
She went and washed that man right outa her hair,
She went and washed that man right outa her hair,
   (NELLIE *joining them in a triumphant finish*)
And sent him on his way!
   (NELLIE *starts to dry her hair with a towel.* EMILE *enters. She cannot see him because the towel covers her eyes. The other girls quickly slip away to leave them alone, all except* DINAH, *who goes to her tin tub and takes out her evening dress.* NELLIE *is humming and dancing as she dries her hair. Suddenly, she stops. She has seen something on the ground—*EMILE's *shoe tops! She moves closer to them, holding the towel forward, as a photographer holds his cloth. She patters over to* DINAH *for confirmation, still holding the towel in this manner.* DINAH *nods, as if to say: "That's him, all right."* NELLIE *makes a dash for the shower. While* NELLIE *is putting*

a top-piece on over her bathing bra, DINAH *stands in front of the shower enclosure, blocking the way, and trying to make conversation with* EMILE. *She looks and feels very silly.*)

DINAH

You'd never think this was an evening dress, would you? We're only allowed to bring two of them—evening dresses . . . only two . . . I brought . . . Yeah, sister!

(*She retreats offstage, with no grace whatever.* NELLIE *comes out of the shower and makes a naive attempt to appear surprised.*)

NELLIE

Hello!

EMILE

Hello. . . . That song . . . is it a new American song?

NELLIE

It's an American type song. We were kind of putting in our own words. (*Looking around*) Where *is* everybody?

EMILE

It is strange with your American songs. In all of them one is either desirous to get rid of one's lover, or one weeps for a man one cannot have.

NELLIE

That's right.

EMILE

I like a song that says: "I love you and you love me . . . And isn't that fine?"

75

NELLIE

(*Not very bright at the moment*)

Yes . . . that's fine.

EMILE

I left a note for you at the hospital. It was to ask you to my home for dinner next Friday.

NELLIE

Well, I don't think I'll be able to come, Emile, I—

EMILE

I have asked all my friends. The planters' colony.

NELLIE

(*Determined to wash him out of her hair*)

A big party. Well then, if I can't come, you won't miss me.

EMILE

But it is *for* you. It is for my friends to meet you and— more important—for you to meet them; to give you an idea of what your life would be like here. I want you to know more about me . . . how I live and think—

NELLIE

(*Suddenly remembering her promise to "spy on him"*)

More about you?

EMILE

Yes. You know very little about me.

NELLIE

That's right! (*Getting down to business*) Would you sit

76

down? (EMILE *sits.* NELLIE *paces like a cross-examiner*) Do you think about politics much . . . And if so what do you think about politics?

EMILE

Do you mean my political philosophy?

NELLIE

I think that's what I mean.

EMILE

Well, to begin with, I believe in the free life—in freedom for everyone.

NELLIE

(*Eagerly*)

Like in the Declaration of Independence?

EMILE

C'est ça. All men are created equal, isn't it?

NELLIE

Emile! You really believe that?

EMILE

Yes.

NELLIE

(*With great relief*)

Well, thank goodness!

EMILE

It is why I am here. . . . Why I killed a man.

77

NELLIE

(Brought back to her mission)

Oh, yes. I meant to ask you about that too . . . I don't want you to think I'm prying into your private life, asking a lot of questions. But . . . I always think it's interesting why a person . . . kills another person.

(EMILE *smiles understandingly.*)

EMILE

Of course, Nellie. That has worried you. (*He turns away to compose his story. Then he begins by stating what he considers the explanation and excuse for the whole thing:*) When I was a boy, I carried my heart in my hand. . . . So . . . when this man came to our town—though my father said he was good—I thought he was bad. (*With a shrug and a smile*) I was young . . . He attracted all the mean and cruel people to him. Soon he was running our town! He could do anything—take anything . . . I did not like that. I was young. (NELLIE *nods, understanding*) I stood up in the public square and made a speech. I called upon everyone to stand with me against this man.

NELLIE

What did they do?

EMILE

(Letting his hands fall helplessly to his side)

They walked away!

NELLIE

Why?

EMILE

Because they saw him standing behind me. I turned, and

78

he said to me, "I am going to kill you now." We fought. I was never so strong. I knocked him to the ground. And when he fell, his head struck a stone and . . . (*He turns away and lets* NELLIE *imagine the rest*) I ran to the waterfront and joined a cargo boat. I didn't even know where it was going. I stepped off that boat into another world . . . (*He looks around him, loving all he sees*) where I am now . . . and where I want to stay. (*He turns to* NELLIE *and impulsively steps toward her, deep sincerity and anxiety in his voice*) Nellie, will you marry me? . . . There are so few days in our life, Nellie. The time I have with you now is precious to me . . . Have you been thinking?

NELLIE

I have been thinking.
(*Singing, thoughtful, considering*)
Born on the opposite sides of the sea,
We are as different as people can be,

EMILE

It's true.

NELLIE

And yet you want to marry me. . . .

EMILE

I do.

NELLIE

I've known you a few short weeks and yet
Somehow you've made my heart forget
All other men I have ever met
But you . . . but you . . .

79

EMILE

Some enchanted evening
You may see a stranger,
You may see a stranger
Across a crowded room,
And somehow you know,
You know even then
That somewhere you'll see her
Again and again. . . .

NELLIE

Who can explain it?
Who can tell you why?

EMILE

Fools give you reasons,
Wise men never try . . .
Some enchanted evening,
When you find your true love,
When you feel her call you
Across a crowded room,
Then fly to her side
And make her your own,
Or all through your life you may dream all alone!

NELLIE

(Clinging to him)
Once you have found him
Never let him go.

EMILE

Once you have found her

80

Never let her go.
  (*They kiss*)
Will you come next Friday?

NELLIE
  (*Somewhere, from out of the ether, she hears her
  voice murmur an inarticulate but automatic assent*)
Uh-huh.
  (EMILE *kisses her again and leaves. There is the sound
  of a girl's laughter offstage and a voice is heard.*)

GIRL'S VOICE
(*Offstage*)
Well, she sure washed him out of her hair!
  (*More laughter.* NELLIE *looks defiantly off in the direc-
  tion of her mocking friends.*)

NELLIE
(*Singing*)
I expect every one
Of my crowd to make fun
Of my proud protestations of faith in romance,
And they'll say I'm naive
As a babe to believe
Any fable I hear from a person in pants! . . .

Fearlessly I'll face them and argue their doubts away,
Loudly I'll sing about flowers and spring!
Flatly I'll stand on my little flat feet and say,
"Love is a grand and a beautiful thing!"
I'm not ashamed to reveal the world-famous feeling I feel.

I'm as corny as Kansas in August,
I'm as normal as blueberry pie.
No more a smart
Little girl with no heart,
I have found me a wonderful guy.

I am in a conventional dither
With a conventional star in my eye
And, you will note,
There's a lump in my throat
When I speak of that wonderful guy.

I'm as trite and as gay
As a daisy in May
(A cliché coming true!)
I'm bromidic and bright
As a moon-happy night
Pouring light on the dew.

I'm as corny as Kansas in August,
High as a flag on the Fourth of July!
If you'll excuse
An expression I use,
I'm in love
I'm in love
I'm in love
I'm in love
I'm in love with a wonderful guy!

> (*The other nurses enter and join in her song; each
> obviously thinking of her own wonderful guy. The
> "company street" curtain closes as they sing, and before*

*the light on the girls fades out, the men are seen pursu-
ing the activities which have characterized previous
company street scenes. The music of "I'm in Love with
a Wonderful Guy" has continued and now the nurses
enter and resume singing it.* NELLIE *running on last and
finishing in a triumphant coda to the amusement of
the G.I.'s. The lights fade on them all as they exit and
the next scene is revealed.)*

ACT ONE

Scene VIII

This is BRACKETT'S *office again.*

BRACKETT, HARBISON *and* CABLE *are all looking intently at* EMILE . . .

BRACKETT

Now, before you give us your answer, I want to impress you with three things. First, you are a civilian and you don't have to go. There's no way of our making you go. Second, this is a very dangerous mission and there's no guarantee that you'll survive—or that it will do any good. Third, that it might do a great good. It might be the means of turning the tide of war in this area.

EMILE

I understand all these things.

BRACKETT

Are you ready to give us your answer?

EMILE

Yes, I am. (*Pause*) My answer must be no. (CABLE's *foot comes down from the top of the waste-basket, on which it was resting.* HARBISON *uncrosses his arms.* BRACKETT *and* HARBISON *exchange looks*) When a man faces death, he must weigh values very carefully. He must weigh the sweetness of his

84

life against the thing he is asked to die for. The probability of death is very great—for both of us. I know that island well, Lieutenant Cable. I am not certain that I believe that what you ask me to do is . . . is—

BRACKETT

We're asking you to help us lick the Japs. It's as simple as that. We're against the Japs.

EMILE

I know what you're against. What are you for? (*He waits for an answer. They have none*) When I was twenty-two, I thought the world hated bullies as much as I did. I was foolish—I killed one. And I was forced to flee to an island. Since then, I have asked no help from anyone or any country. I have seen these bullies multiply and grow strong. The world sat by and watched.

CABLE

Aw, to hell with this, de Becque, let's be honest! Aren't you just a guy in love with a girl and you're putting her above everything else in the world?

(EMILE *looks at* CABLE *for a moment before answering.*)

EMILE

Yes, I do care about my life with her more than anything else in the world. It is the only thing that is important to me. This I believe in. This I am sure of. This I have. I cannot risk to lose it. Good day, gentlemen.

(*He goes out. There is a pause. All three men have been rocked off their balance.*)

85

HARBISON
(*Thoughtfully*)

He's an honest man, but he's wrong. Of course, we can't guarantee him a better world if we win. Point is, we can be damned sure it'll be worse if we lose. Can't we? . . . (*Hotly*) Well, can't we?

BRACKETT
(*Rising*)

Of course. Cable, there's a bottle of Scotch in my bottom drawer. See you tomorrow.

(*He exits quickly.* HARBISON *goes to the desk and takes a bottle from a drawer.*)

HARBISON

This is the one he means.

(*He takes two glasses and starts to pour the Scotch. A* YEOMAN *enters holding a sheaf of papers to be signed.*)

YEOMAN
(*Querulously*)

Commander Harbison! The Old Man walked right out on me with all these orders to be signed! And there's another delegation of French planters here, complaining about that stolen pig—the one the Seabees took and barbecued. And Commander Hutton's here—

HARBISON
(*Grabbing papers from him, irritably*)

Okay, okay! . . . I'll take care of it!

YEOMAN

Well, all right, sir!

CABLE

(*As he takes his glass of Scotch*)
What should I do, Commander Harbison? Go back to my
outfit tonight?

HARBISON

(*With his drink in his hand*)
No, take a couple days off and unwind.

CABLE

Unwind?

HARBISON

Sure. Take a boat. Go fishing.

CABLE

(*A light dawning on him, a memory of* BILLIS' *offer and*
BLOODY MARY'S *song about Bali Ha'i*)
Boat!
(*He puts his glass down and exits suddenly—as if
pulled out of the room!* HARBISON *takes a swallow of
Scotch, puts down his glass, looks around for* CABLE,
but CABLE *has disappeared.* HARBISON *rubs his face with
the gesture of a weary man, and starts to go to work on
the papers as the lights fade.*)

ACT ONE

Scene IX

As BRACKETT'S *office recedes upstage, the tapa-cloth curtain closes and groups of French girls and native girls enter. They sing softly:*

GIRLS

Bali ha'i t'appele
Dans le jour,
Dans la nuit.
Dans ton coeur,
Toujours resonne,
Par ici,
Me voici.
Si tu veux,
Tu me trouvera
Ou le ciel
Trouve la mer.
Me voici,
Laisse moi te prendre
Par ici,
Me voici,
Bali ha'i,
    Bali ha'i,
        Bali ha'i!

(*There is a bell ringing offstage. A native* KID *shouts excitedly,* "Boat! Boat! Boat!" *He runs off left. The girls*

88

back away a few steps as BILLIS, CABLE *and* BLOODY MARY
walk on.)

CABLE
(*As he enters*)
Look, Billis, I didn't come over here to Bali Ha'i to see
anybody cut any boar's teeth out.

BILLIS
It ain't the cutting of the boar's tooth exactly. It's what
comes afterwards.
(*During these lines,* MARY *has whispered into a small
boy's ear and sent him running off.* CABLE *has crossed
the girls and looks back over his shoulder at them.*)

MARY
(*Smiling, understanding perfectly*)
I take you with me. Come, Lootellan. You have good time.
(*Calling to a native*) Marcel! Come here! Billis, Marcel take
you to boar ceremony. Lootellan come later. (*Two French
girls have caught* CABLE's *eye, and he has about made up his
mind to approach them. He takes a couple of steps toward
them, but now two* NUNS *enter and engage them in conversation. Thwarted by this unhappy development,* CABLE *becomes
more receptive to* MARY, *who now says:*) Lootellan, come with
me. You have good time. Come!
(*She leads him off as the lights fade.*)

ACT ONE

Scene X

The music swells. A concentration of light in the center of the stage reveals:

The interior of a native hut.

BLOODY MARY *comes in. Even she has to bend low to get through the doorway.* CABLE, *following her, finds himself in the darkness, blinking.*

CABLE

What's this?

MARY

You wait.

CABLE

There's nobody around here.

MARY

You wait, Lootellan.

CABLE

What's going on, Mary? What—
   (*He doesn't finish because a small figure has appeared in the doorway. A girl, perhaps seventeen. Her black hair is drawn smooth over her head. Like* BLOODY MARY, *she wears a white blouse and black trousers. Barefooted, she stands, silent, shy and motionless against the wattled wall, looking at* CABLE *with the honest curiosity and admiration of a child.*)

MARY

(To CABLE, *with a sly smile)*

You like?

CABLE

(Never taking his eyes from the girl)

Who is she?

MARY

Liat.

LIAT

(Nodding her head and repeating it in a small voice)

Liat.

MARY

Is French name.

CABLE

(Still stunned, still gazing at the girl)

Liat.

MARY

But she no French girl. She Tonkinese like me. We are ver' pretty people— No? . . .

(She goes closer to CABLE *and looks at him. She turns to* LIAT *and then back to* CABLE. *The two young people continue to regard each other with silent, longing interest.)*

CABLE

(Over MARY's *head, to* LIAT)

Do you speak English?

MARY

Only a few word. She talk French. *(To* LIAT) Français!

91

LIAT
(Smiling shyly)

Je parle Français—un peu.
(She holds her forefinger and thumb close together to show how very little French she speaks.)

CABLE
(Grinning, nearly as shy as she)

Moi, aussi—un peu. *(He holds up his forefinger and thumb, just as she did. They both laugh, and in some strange way, BLOODY MARY seems to have been forgotten by both of them. She looks from one to the other. Then, with the air of one who has accomplished a purpose, she waddles to the doorway. As she goes out, she lets the bamboo curtain roll down across the opening, reducing the light inside the hut. There is a long moment of silence)* Are you afraid of me? *(LIAT looks puzzled. He remembers she knows only a few words of English)* Oh . . . er . . . avez-vous peur?

LIAT
(Her young face serious)

Non. *(He takes a step toward her. She backs closer to the wall)* Oui! *(He stops and looks at her, worried and hurt. This sign of gentleness wins her. She smiles)* . . . Non.
(Now it is she who walks slowly toward him. The music builds in a rapturous upsurge. CABLE gathers LIAT in his arms. She reaches her small arms up to his neck. He lifts her off her feet. The lights fade slowly as his hand slides her blouse up her back toward her shoulders. The lights dim to complete darkness. Light projections of large and lovely Oriental blossoms are

thrown against the drop. Native couples stroll across the stage, only dimly seen. The music mounts ecstatically, then diminishes. The stage is clear. The light comes up on the hut again and moonlight now comes through the opened doorway where CABLE *stands. He has no shirt on.* LIAT *is seated on the floor, gazing up at him silently; her hair hangs loose down her back.* CABLE *smiles down at her.*)

CABLE

(*Trying to puzzle something out in his mind*)

But you're just a kid . . . How did that Bloody Mary get a kid like you to come here and . . . I don't get it! (*Suddenly realizing that she has not understood*) Cette vielle femme . . . votre amie?

LIAT

Ma mère.

CABLE

(*Horrified*)

Your mother! Bloody Mary is your mother! But she didn't tell me.

(LIAT, *to divert him from unpleasant thoughts, suddenly throws herself in his lap; they kiss. The sound of a ship's bell is heard in the distance. They sit up.* LIAT *looks panic-stricken.*)

LIAT

Non, Non!

(*She covers his ears with her hands.*)

93

(*Looking off*)

It's the boat all right. (*He turns back to her, sees her little face below his, her eyes pleading with him to stay*) Aw, let them wait.

(*He sings*)
I touch your hand
And my arms grow strong,
Like a pair of birds
That burst with song.
My eyes look down
At your lovely face
And I hold the world
In my embrace.

Younger than springtime are you,
Softer than starlight are you,
Warmer than winds of June are the gentle lips you gave me.
Gayer than laughter are you,
Sweeter than music are you,
Angel and lover, heaven and earth are you to me,
And when your youth and joy invade my arms
And fill my heart as now they do,
Then,
Younger than springtime am I,
Gayer than laughter am I,
Angel and lover, heaven and earth am I with you . . .

(*He releases her, goes to the door, looks off, then comes back to her. He stoops to pick up his shirt. She tries to get it first. Each has hold of one end of it. He looks down at her and repeats, softly:*)

94

And when your youth and joy invade my arms
And fill my heart as now they do,
Then, younger than springtime am I,
Gayer than laughter am I
Angel and lover, heaven and earth am I with you.

(*He starts. She clings to her end of his shirt for a
moment, then lets it slide through her sad little fingers,
and watches him go through the door—out of her life,
perhaps. She sinks to her knees. The lights fade. Now,
again in front of the tapa-cloth curtain, native girls
bearing trays of tropical flowers and French girls are
gathered in several groups.*)

ACT ONE

Scene XI

The girls sing and hum "Bali Ha'i" softly under the scene, as Hawaiians sing "Aloha" to all departing craft. BLOODY MARY *and* BILLIS *are looking off, anxiously awaiting* CABLE.

BILLIS

(Shouting off)

Ring the bell again! Ring the bell again! (*Taking a lei from a* FLOWER-SELLER) I'll have another one of those.

(*He drapes the lei around his neck where he already has three others.*)

MARY

He come. He come. He be here soon. Don't worry, Billis.

BILLIS

Hey, Mary— Please ask those Boar Tooth ceremonial fellows not to be sore at me. I didn't think those girls would do a religious dance with only skirts on. If somebody had told me it was a religious dance, I wouldn't have gotten up and danced with them. (*Looking off*) Oh! Here he comes! Here he comes.

(BILLIS *exits toward the boat.* CABLE *enters and crosses the stage in a kind of dream.* MARY *smiles, ecstatic, as she sees his face. Several of the French girls try to flirt with* CABLE, *but he doesn't know they're alive. He goes right by them.* MARY *then walks past them, her chin in the air, very proudly and triumphantly. The girls' voices rise, singing the final measures of "Bali Ha'i." They throw flowers offstage where* BILLIS *and* CABLE *made their exit. Cries of "Au revoir" and laughter are heard over the singing.)*

MARY
(Throwing flower garland she has taken from a native girl and shouting to the others)
Is gonna be my son-in-law. *(Calling off)* Goo' bye! Come back soon, Lootellan! Bali Ha'i! Come back soon!

The lights fade.

ACT ONE

Scene XII

And other lights come up slowly on EMILE's *terrace.*

The good-byes continue through the darkness and other good-byes from other voices blend in with these . . . all in French.

HENRY enters with another SERVANT. *They start to clear glasses, champagne bottles and other left-overs of a gay party which clutter the scene.*

FRENCHMAN
(Offstage)

Bali Ha'i . . . Bon soir!

FRENCHWOMAN
(Offstage)

Merci, Emile. Merci, mille fois!
(EMILE *enters and addresses* HENRY.)

EMILE

Pas maintenant . . . demain!

FRENCHMAN
(Offstage)

A bientot! Bali Ha'i.
(HENRY *and the other servant exit.*)

98

FRENCHWOMAN
(*Offstage*)

Quelle charmante soirée.

NELLIE
(*Offstage*)

Good night . . . everybody . . . Good night.

FRENCHMAN
(*Offstage*)

Non, Non . . . Nellie . . . en Français . . . en Français.

NELLIE
(*Offstage, laboring with her French*)

Je . . . suis . . . enchantée . . . de faire . . . votre . . . connaissance!

(EMILE, *looking off, smiles with amusement and pride. Voices offstage shout "Bravo!" "Formidable!"* EMILE *exits.*)

FRENCHMAN
(*Offstage*)

Bon soir, de Becque.

FRENCHWOMAN
(*Offstage*)

Merci mille fois!!!

(*There is the sound of a motor starting loud, then growing fainter.* EMILE *and* NELLIE *enter and turn back to wave good-bye to the last guests. Then* NELLIE *turns to* EMILE, *who has been gently urging her farther into the garden. There is high excitement in her voice and she speaks very rapidly.*)

NELLIE

Emile, you know I can't stay. And I've got to get that jeep back. I stole it. Or rather, I borrowed it. Or rather a fellow stole it for me. A wonderful man named Billis. I'll have to sneak around behind the hospital as it is.

EMILE

In that case, I forbid you to go! If you have to sneak back without anyone seeing you, you might just as well sneak back later.

(NELLIE *thinks for an instant, then comes to a quick decision.*)

NELLIE
(*Taking off her coat*)

You're absolutely right! (*She looks guiltily at* EMILE *and screams with laughter. So does he. She puts her coat on the back of a chair*) I never had such a wonderful time in my whole life. All these lovely people and that cute old man who spoke French with me and made believe he understood me. And that exciting native couple who danced for us. Oh, it's so different from *Little Rock!* (*She screams the last line passionately, as if she hopes Little Rock would hear.* EMILE *laughs uproariously. She suddenly becomes quiet:*) What on earth are you laughing at? Am I drunk?

EMILE
(*Still laughing*)

Oh, no.

NELLIE

Yes, I am. But it isn't the champagne—it's because I'm in love with a wonderful guy!

(She sings this last line. They waltz to the music of "I'm in Love with a Wonderful Guy!" NELLIE resumes singing)

If you'll excuse an expression I use,
I'm in love, I'm in love, I'm in love—

EMILE

(Also singing)

I'm in love, I'm in love and the girl that I love—She thinks I'm a wonderful guy!

(They stop, exhausted and laughing. She turns and notices a half-filled glass of champagne which has been left by one of the guests. She takes it up and drinks it.)

NELLIE

Imagine leaving all this wonderful champagne! *(She drinks out of this one, then takes another one. She hands it to EMILE)* Here, Emile. You have some, too. It's such a waste!

EMILE

Here—here's another bottle.

(He goes over to a long table which is under the windows on the porch. There are several buckets of champagne there. He takes one and fills two clean glasses and brings them to NELLIE. Meanwhile, she leans back, stretching her arms behind her head. Dreamily, she sings:)

101

NELLIE

This is how it feels,
Living on a hillside . . .

(She speaks as the melody in the orchestra continues)
Here we are just like two old married people. Our guests
have gone home and we're alone.

EMILE

(Handing her the glass of champagne, singing:)
This is what I need,
This is what I've longed for—
Someone young and smiling,
Here upon my hill—

*(The orchestra starts the music of "A Cockeyed Opti-
mist."* NELLIE *has been thinking.)*

NELLIE

Emile, you know, my mother says we have nothing in
common. But she's wrong. We have something very important in common—very much in common.

EMILE

Yes, we're both in love.

NELLIE

Yes, but more than that. We're—we're the same kind of
people fundamentally—you and me. We appreciate things!
We get enthusiastic about things. It's really quite exciting
when two people are like that. We're not blasé. You know
what I mean?

EMILE

We're both knuckleheads, cockeyed optimists.
   (*They both laugh and start to sing:*)

NELLIE

I hear the human race
Is falling on its face . . .

EMILE

And hasn't very far to go!

NELLIE

But every whippoorwill
Is selling me a bill
And telling me it just ain't so.

BOTH

   (*Harmonizing—"Sweet Adeline" fashion*)
I could say life is just a bowl of jello
And appear more intelligent and smart,
But I'm stuck,
Like a dope,
With a thing called hope,
And I can't get it out of my heart . . .
   (*Dwelling on the fancy ending:*)
Not this heart!
   (*They smile in each other's eyes.* EMILE *suddenly gets
   an idea and rises.*)

EMILE

Nellie, I have a surprise for you. You sit over there—something that I have been preparing for two days. Close your eyes. No peeking.

(EMILE *looks around first for a prop, sees her coat, then makes her go over and sit by the fountain.* NELLIE *is mystified, but excited, like a child waiting for a surprise.* EMILE *takes her coat and throwing it over his head, using it to simulate a towel, he imitates her as he found her on the beach the other day*)

I'm going to wash that man right out of my hair,
I'm going to wash that man right out of my hair,

NELLIE

Oh, no! No!
(*She writhes with embarrassment and laughter as he continues:*)

EMILE

I'm going to wash that man right out of my hair
And send him on his way! . . .
(*She covers her eyes*)
Don't try to patch it up,
Tear it up, tear it up,
Wash him out, dry him out,
Push him out, fly him out,
Cancel him, and let him go—
Yea, Sister!
(*He finishes, waving his arms wildly.*)

NELLIE
(*Applauding*)
That's wonderful, Emile.
(EMILE *lifts the coat and, looking off, sees* NGANA *and*

JEROME *as they enter in their nightgowns, followed by* HENRY.)

EMILE

Bon soir!
(NELLIE *turns, looks at the children and is immediately enchanted. She kneels before the two of them, holding them at arm's length.*)

NELLIE

You're the cutest things I ever saw in my whole life! What are your names? You probably can't understand a word I'm saying, but, oh, my goodness, you're cute.

EMILE

Nellie, I want you to meet Ngana and Jerome. Ngana and Jerome, Nellie.

NGANA AND JEROME

Nellie . . .

EMILE
(To the children)
Maintenant au lit . . . vite!

HENRY

Venez, Petits!

NGANA

Bon soir, Nellie.

JEROME

Bon soir, Nellie.
(*They wave to* NELLIE, *as* HENRY *leads them out.*)

NELLIE

Bon soir! (*Turning to* EMILE) Oh, aren't they adorable! Those big black eyes staring at you out of those sweet little faces! Are they Henry's?

EMILE

They're mine.

NELLIE

(*Carrying out what she thinks is a joke*)
Oh, of course, they look exactly like you, don't they? Where did you hide their mother?

EMILE

She's dead, Nellie.

NELLIE

She's— (*She turns*) Emile, they *are* yours!

EMILE

Yes, Nellie. I'm their father.

NELLIE

And—their mother . . . was a . . . was . . . a . . .

EMILE

Polynesian. (NELLIE *is stunned. She turns away, trying to collect herself*) And she was beautiful, Nellie, and charming, too.

NELLIE

But you and she . . .

106

EMILE

I want you to know I have no apologies. I came here as a young man. I lived as I could.

NELLIE

Of course.

EMILE

But I have not been selfish. No woman ever hated me or tried to hurt me.

NELLIE

No woman could ever want to hurt you, Emile. (*Suddenly, feeling she must get away as quickly as she can*) Oh, what time is it? I promised to get that jeep back! (*She looks at her wrist watch*) Oh, this is awful. Look at the time!
(*She grabs her coat.* EMILE *tries to stop her.*)

EMILE

Nellie, wait, please. I'll drive you home.

NELLIE

You will do no such thing. Anyway, I couldn't leave the jeep here. I've got to get it back by—

EMILE

Don't go now, Nellie. Don't go yet, please.

NELLIE

(*Rattling on very fast*)

Yes, I must go now. This is terrible! I won't be able to face the girls at the hospital. You can't imagine the way they look at you when you come in late . . . I'll call you, Emile.

I'll come by tomorrow. (*Suddenly remembering*) Oh, no! Oh, dear! There are those awful rehearsals for Thanksgiving Day—I'm teaching them a dance and they want to rehearse night and day—but after that— (*Shifting quickly*) Oh, thank you for tonight, Emile. I had a wonderful time. It was the nicest party and you're a perfect host. Good-bye. Please stay here, Emile. Don't go out to the jeep, please.

EMILE

(*Grabbing her arms, feeling her slipping away from him*) Nellie, I love you. Do you hear me, Nellie? I love you!

NELLIE

And I love you, too. Honestly I do— Please let me go! Please let me go!

> (NELLIE *goes off. She runs as fast as she can.* EMILE *watches for a second. The motor of the jeep starts and fades away quickly, as though the jeep were driven away very, very fast. The music of "Some Enchanted Evening" swells as* EMILE *looks down and picks up a coffee cup that has been left on the fountain.*)

EMILE

(*Singing, as he looks down at the cup*)
Once you have found her,
Never let her go.
Once you have found her,
Never let her go!

Curtain

ACT TWO

ACT TWO

Scene I

The stage during a performance of "The Thanksgiving Follies."

A dance is in progress, four girls and four boys. NELLIE *is one of the girls. They meticulously perform the steps and evolutions of a dance routine no more distinguished or original than any that might be produced by a Navy nurse who had been the moving spirit in the amateur theatre of Little Rock. Not one of the dancers makes a single mistake. Nobody smiles. Tense concentration is evident in this laboriously perfect performance. During the course of the dance, there are solo "step-outs" after which each soloist soberly steps back into place. The most complicated unison step is saved for the exit, which they execute with vigorous precision.*

On either side, in the downstage corners of the stage, G.I.'s are sitting as if there had not been enough seats and the audience overflowed up onto the stage. There are no chairs. They are seated and sprawled on the floor of the stage.

NELLIE *returns to the stage, a sheaf of notes in her hand and talks into the microphone.*

NELLIE

It has been called to our attention that owing to some trouble with the mimeograph, the last part of the program is kind of blurry, so I will read off who did the last number.

III

(*Reading*) The hand-stand was by Marine Sergeant Johnson. (*Applause*) The Barrel Roll was done by Lieutenant J. G. Bessie May Sue Ellie Jaeger. (*Applause*) The solo featuring the hitch-kick and scissors . . . those are the names of the steps . . . was by Ensign Cora McRae. (*Applause*) The Pin Wheel . . . you know—(*She demonstrates by waving her leg in imitation of* STEWPOT) was by Stewpot . . . I mean George Watts, Carpenter's Mate, Third Class.

(*Applause.* STEWPOT's *head protrudes from the wings.*)

STEWPOT

Second class.

(*Applause.*)

NELLIE

The multiple revolutions and—(NELLIE *becomes self-consciously modest*) incidentally the dance steps were by Ensign Nellie Forbush. (*She bows. Applause*) Now the next is a most unusual treat. An exhibition of weight lifting by Marine Staff Sergeant Thomas Hassinger.

(HASSINGER *enters from right. He flexes muscles. Applause and shouts from "audience" on the corner of the stage.*)

SAILOR

Atta boy, Muscles!

(*The lights start fading.*)

NELLIE

. . . and Sergeant Johnson . . . (JOHNSON *enters*) Marine Corporal . . .

(*The lights are out.*)

VOICE IN DARK

Hey, lights . . . the lights are out . . . Billis!

NELLIE

Bill-is . . . what the heck happened to the lights?

OTHER VOICES

"It's the generator." "Generator ran out of gas." "Switch over to the other one." "Mike . . . turn on the truck lights."

NELLIE

Keep your seats, everybody! There's nothing wrong except that the lights went out.

VOICES

"Look where you're going." "How the hell can I look when I can't see?"

(The lights come up. The set has been changed in the darkness. We are now in:)

ACT TWO

In back of the stage.

SEABEE

We'll have that other generator on in a minute.

BILLIS

They got the truck lights on. That's something.
(*Applause offstage, right.*)

STEWPOT

(*Looking off toward "stage"*)
The weight-lifting act got started.

BILLIS

Good . . . (*He notices two Seabees who are pushing a large roll of cable*) What I can't understand is how some guys ain't got the artistic imagination to put gas in a generator so a show can be a success . . . especially when they're on the committee.

FIRST SEABEE

You're on the committee, too. Why didn't you tell us it wasn't gassed up?

BILLIS

I'm acting in the show and I'm stage manager and producer. I can't figure out everything, can I?

SECOND SEABEE

Sure you can. Just put your two heads together.
(*He and his companion exit, pushing the roll of cable before them.*)

BILLIS

(*Calling off*)

Look, jerk! I got a production on my hands. (*Turning to* STEWPOT) How's the weight-lifting act going?

STEWPOT

I can't tell. Nobody's clapping.

BILLIS

If nobody's clapping, they ain't going good. You ought to be able to figure that out. Put your two heads together.

STEWPOT

You was the one with two heads.
(EMILE *enters. He carries a bunch of flowers in his hand. He has a serious "set" expression in his eyes.*)

Pardon, can you tell me where I can find Miss Forbush?

BILLIS

(*Shrewdly sensing trouble and determined to protect* NELLIE)

She's on stage now. She's the Emcee. She can't talk to nobody right now. Do you want me to take the flowers in to her?

EMILE

No. I would prefer to give them to her myself.

BILLIS

Are you Mister de Becque?

EMILE

Yes.

BILLIS

Look, Mister de Becque. Do me a favor, will you? Don't try and see her tonight.

EMILE

Why?

BILLIS

We got her in a great mood tonight and I don't want anything to upset her again.

EMILE

She has been upset?

BILLIS

Upset! She's asked for a transfer to another island. And day before yesterday, she busted out crying right in the middle of rehearsal. Said she couldn't go on with the show. And she wouldn't have either unless Captain Brackett talked to her and told her how important it was to the Base. So do us all a favor—don't try to see her now.

EMILE

She's asked for a transfer?

BILLIS

Don't tell her I told you. Nobody's supposed to know.

116

EMILE

I must see her. Tonight!

BILLIS

Then stay out of sight till after the show. I'll take the flowers to her.

(EMILE *gives him the flowers.* BILLIS *and* STEWPOT *exit.* CABLE *enters. He doesn't see* EMILE *at first.*)

CABLE

Hey, Billis— Billis!

EMILE

(Peering through the semi-darkness)
Lieutenant Cable?

CABLE

(Putting his fingers to his lips in a mocking gesture)
Ssh! Lieutenant Cable is supposed to be in his little bed over at the hospital.

EMILE

You have not been well?

CABLE

I'm okay now. Fever gone. They can't hold me in that damned place any longer. I'm looking for a guy named Billis, a great guy for getting boats. *(His voice rising, tense and shrill)* And I need a boat right now. I've got to get to my island.

EMILE

(Worried by CABLE's *strangeness)*
What?

CABLE

That damned island with the two volcanoes on it. You ever been over there?

EMILE

Why, yes, I—

CABLE

I went over there every day till this damned malaria stopped me. Have you sailed over early in the morning? With warm rain playing across your face? (LIAT *enters. He sees her, but doesn't believe his eyes*) Beginning to see her again like last night.

LIAT
(*Calling offstage*)

Ma mère! C'est lui!
(*She turns and, like a young deer, glides over to the amazed* CABLE *and embraces him before the equally amazed* EMILE. MARY *waddles on.*)

CABLE
(*Holding* LIAT *tight*)

I thought I was dreaming.

LIAT
(*Laughing*)

Non.
(*She holds him tighter.*)

CABLE
(*He holds her away from him and looks at her*)

What are you doing over here?

118

MARY

(*Grimly*)

She come in big white boat—bigger than your boat. Belong Jacques Barrere. He want to marry Liat. (*To* EMILE) You know him. (EMILE *nods. She turns back to* CABLE) Is white man, too. And very rich!

CABLE

(*To* LIAT)

Is that the old planter you told me about? The one who drinks? (*His eye catches* EMILE's. EMILE *nods.* CABLE *cries out as if hurt*) Oh, my God! (*He turns angrily to* MARY) You can't let her marry a man like that.

MARY

Hokay! Then *you* marry her.

EMILE

(*Angrily, to* MARY)

Tais-toi! Il est malade! . . . Tu comprends? (MARY *is temporarily silenced.* EMILE *turns to* CABLE *and his voice becomes gentle and sympathetic*) Lieutenant, I am worried about you. You are ill. Will you allow me to see you back to the hospital?

CABLE

You're worried about me! That's funny. The fellow who says he lives on an island all by himself and doesn't worry about anybody—Japs, Americans, Germans—anybody. Why pick out *me* to worry about?

119

EMILE
(Stiffly)

Forgive me. I'm sorry, Lieutenant.

(*He leaves.* MARY *goes to* CABLE *to make one last plea for her daughter's dream.*)

MARY

Lootellan, you like Liat. . . . Marry Liat! You have good life here. Look, Lootellan, I am rich. I save six hundred dolla' before war. Since war I make two thousand dolla' . . . war go on I make maybe more. Sell grass skirts, boar's teeth, real human heads. Give all de money to you an' Liat. You no have to work. I work for you. . . . (*Soft music is played*) All day long, you and Liat be together! Walk through woods, swim in sea, sing, dance, talk happy. No think about Philadelia. Is no good. Talk about beautiful things and make love all day long. You like? You buy?

(*She sings. Throughout the song,* LIAT *performs what seem to be traditional gestures*)

Happy Talk,
Keep talkin' Happy Talk!
Talk about tings you'd like to do.
You got to have a dream—
If you don' have a dream
How you gonna have a dream come true?

Talk about a moon
Floatin' in de sky,
Lookin' like a lily on a lake:
Talk about a bird

Learnin' how to fly,
Makin' all de music he can make.

Happy Talk,
Keep talkin' Happy Talk!
Talk about tings you'd like to do.
You got to have a dream—
If you don' have a dream
How you gonna have a dream come true?

Talk about a star
Lookin' like a toy,
Peekin' through de branches of a tree.
Talk about a girl,
Talk about a boy
Countin' all de ripples on de sea.

Happy Talk,
Keep talkin' Happy Talk!
Talk about tings you'd like to do.
You got to have a dream—
If you don' have a dream
How you gonna have a dream come true?
> (LIAT *now performs a gentle, childish dance. At the end
> of it, she returns to* CABLE's *side and* MARY *resumes her
> song:*)

Talk about a boy
Sayin' to de girl,
"Golly, baby, I'm a lucky cuss!"
Talk about a girl
Saying to de boy,

"You an' me is lucky to be us."

(LIAT *and* CABLE *kiss.* MARY'S *voice becomes triumphant*)

Happy Talk,
Keep talkin' Happy Talk!
Talk about tings you'd like to do.
You got to have a dream—
If you don' have a dream
How you gonna have a dream come true?

If you don' talk happy
An' you never have a dream
Den you'll never have a dream come true.

(*Speaking eagerly*)

Is good idea . . . you like?

(*She laughs gaily and looks in* CABLE'S *eyes, anxious to see the answer.* CABLE *is deeply disturbed. He takes a gold watch from his pocket and puts it in* LIAT'S *hand.*)

CABLE

Liat, I want you to have this. It's a man's watch but it's a good one—belonged to my grandfather. It's kind of a lucky piece, too. My dad carried it all through the last war. Beautiful, isn't it?

(LIAT *has taken the watch, her eyes gleaming with pride.*)

MARY

When I see you firs' time. I know you good man for Liat. And she good girl for you. You have special good babies.

(*Pause.* CABLE *looks tortured.*)

CABLE

(*Forcing the words out*)

Mary, I can't . . . marry . . . Liat.

MARY

(*Letting out her rage and disappointment in a shout, as she grabs* LIAT's *arm*)

Was your las' chance! Now she marry Jacques Barrere. Come, Liat! (LIAT *runs to* CABLE. MARY *pulls her away*) Give me watch. (LIAT *clasps it tight in her hands.* MARY *wrests it from her and yells at* CABLE) Stingy bastard!

(*She throws it on the ground and it smashes.* CABLE *looks on, dazed, stunned.* MARY *pulls* LIAT *off.* CABLE *kneels down, gathers up the pieces and puts them in his pocket. Meanwhile, several of the men come on, dressed for the finale of the show. They are looking back over their shoulders at* LIAT *and* MARY *whom they must have just passed.*)

PROFESSOR

Hey! Did you get a load of that little Tonkinese girl?

(*They continue up to the stage door as they speak.*)

MARINE

Yeah.

(*Applause off.* NELLIE's *voice is heard through the loud-speaker.*)

NELLIE

(*Offstage*)

Now, boys, before we come to the last act of our show,

it is my great pleasure to bring you our skipper, Captain George Brackett.

> (*Applause.* CABLE *looks off at* LIAT *as she passes out of his life.*)

CABLE

(*Singing*)

Younger than springtime were you,
Softer than starlight were you,
Angel and lover, heaven and earth
Were you to me. . . .

ACT TWO

Scene III

The lights fade to complete darkness. BRACKETT'S *voice is heard in the loudspeaker. During his speech, the lights come up, revealing:*

The G.I. Stage, as before. BRACKETT *is speaking into a microphone.*

BRACKETT

Up to now, our side has been having the hell beat out of it in two hemispheres and we're not going to get to go home until that situation is reversed. It may take a long time before we can get any big operation under way, so it's things like this, like this show tonight, that keep us going. Now I understand that I am not generally considered a sentimental type. (*Laughter and cries of "Oh, boy!" "Check," "You can say that again," etc., from the boys on the corners of the stage*) Once or twice I understand I have been referred to as "Old Iron Belly."

VOICES

"Once or twice." "Just about a million times."
(*Loud laughter.*)

BRACKETT

I resent that very much because I had already chosen that as my private name for our Executive Officer, Commander

125

Harbison. (*Big laugh. Applause.* BRACKETT *calls into the wings*)
Take a bow, Commander.

> (*Two of the girls pull* COMMANDER HARBISON *out.*)

SAILOR

I wish I was a commander!

> (HARBISON, *flanked by the two girls, stands beside*
> BRACKETT *as he continues:*)

BRACKETT

I want you to know that both "Old Iron Bellies" sat here
tonight and had a hell of a good time. And we want to thank
that hard working committee of Nurses and Seabees who
made the costumes out of rope and mosquito nets, comic books
and newspapers . . .

> (*He fingers the comic-paper skirt of one of the girls.*)

SAILOR

Ah, ah—captain!

> (BRACKETT *frowns, but pulls himself together.*)

BRACKETT

. . . and thought up these jokes and these grand songs.
And I just want to say on this Thanksgiving Day, to all of
them from all of us, thank you. (*Applause from the boys,
but it is comically feeble. Obviously, they'd like to get on with
the show*) And now I'm going to ask Commander Harbison
to announce the next act which is the Finale of our Thanksgiving entertainment.

> (*He hands* HARBISON *a paper.* HARBISON *reads from a
> small card.*)

HARBISON

The next and last will be a song sung by Bosun Butch
Forbush . . . (*He looks kind of puzzled*) . . . and that Siren
of the Coral Sea . . . gorgeous, voluptuous and petite Mademoiselle Lutheria . . . (*Ending in a high, surprised voice, as
he reads the name of his pet abomination*) . . . Billis!

BRACKETT
(*Laughing*)

Come on, Bill.
(*He leads off* HARBISON, *who is looking at the paper,
puzzled. The music of "Honey-Bun" starts and* NELLIE
*enters, dressed as a sailor, in a borrowed white sailor
suit, three times too big for her.*)

NELLIE
(*Singing*)

My doll is as dainty as a sparrow,
Her figure is something to applaud.
Where she's narrow, she's as narrow as an arrow
And she's broad where a broad should be broad!

A hundred and one
Pounds of fun—
That's my little Honey-Bun!
Get a load of Honey-Bun tonight!

I'm speakin' of my
Sweetie Pie,
Only sixty inches high—
Ev'ry inch is packed with dynamite!

Her hair is blonde and curly,
Her curls are hurly-burly.
Her lips are pips!
I call her hips:
"Twirly"
And "Whirly."
She's my baby,
I'm her Pap!
I'm her booby,
She's my trap!
I am caught and I don't wanta run
'Cause I'm havin' so much fun with Honey-Bun!

> (NELLIE *starts a second refrain, meanwhile having considerable difficulty with her sagging trousers. Now* BILLIS *enters, dressed as a South Sea siren in a straw-colored wig, long lashes fantastically painted on his eyelids, lips painted in bright carmine, two coconut shells on his chest to simulate "femininity" and a battle-ship tatooed on his bare midriff. He and* NELLIE *dance. For an exit, she leads him off, singing a special ending.)*

NELLIE

She's my baby,
I'm her Pap!
I'm her booby,
She's my trap!
I am caught and I don't wanta run
'Cause I'm havin' so much fun with Honey-Bun!
(Believe me, sonny)
She's a cookie who can cook you till you're done,
(Ain't bein' funny)

Sonny,
Put your money
On my Honey-Bun!

> (*After they exit,* NELLIE *returns for a bow. Then* BILLIS
> *enters with* EMILE'S *flowers and presents them to her.
> Thinking they are from* BILLIS, *she kisses him. He exits
> in a delirious daze. She exits as the girls enter, singing.*)

GIRLS

A hundred and one
Pounds of fun—
That's my little Honey-Bun
Get a load of Honey-Bun tonight.

I'm speakin' of my
Sweetie Pie,
Only sixty inches high—
Every inch is packed with dynamite.

> (*The girls are dressed in home-made costumes repre-
> senting island natives. The materials are fish-net, para-
> chute cloth, large tropical leaves and flowers—anything
> they could find and sew together. At the end of their
> line is* BILLIS *still dressed as a girl. As the song proceeds,
> he is the butt of many a slur from his comrades. While
> passing one of them, he is shocked and infuriated to
> feel a hand thrust up his skirt. He turns to swing on
> him, but he can't get out of line and spoil the number;
> "On with the show!" He is grim and stoic—even when
> another boy lifts one of the coconuts in his "brassiere"
> and steals a package of cigarettes therefrom. The girls*

129

and BILLIS *continue singing through these impromptu shenanigans.*)

GIRLS

Her hair is blonde and curly,
Her curls are hurly-burly.
Her lips are pips!
I call her hips:
"Twirly" and "Whirly."

She's my baby,
I'm her Pap!
I'm her booby,
She's my trap!
I am caught and I don't wanta run
'Cause I'm havin' so much fun with Honey-Bun!
        (*All lining up for finale*)
And that's the finish,
And it's time to go for now the show is done.
        (*Balance of* "COMPANY" *comes on*)
We hope you liked us,
And we hope that when you leave your seat and run
Down to the Mess Hall
You'll enjoy your dinner each and every one.
        (NELLIE *makes a special entrance, now wearing a new costume.*)

NELLIE
(*Very brightly*)

Enjoy your turkey.

ALL
(*Pointing to* BILLIS)

And put some chestnut dressing on our Honey-Bun!

(*The curtain is slow.* NELLIE *signals for it and jumps up to help pull it down. The lights are off. Boys on the stage wave their flashlights out at the audience, addressing them as if they were all G.I.'s. "See you down at the mess hall," etc. When the clamor dies down, two lines are distinguishable.*)

SAILOR

How d'ye like the show?

MARINE

It stunk!

ACT TWO

Scene IV

Now the lights come up on the scene behind the stage.
The girls come off the stage and file into their dressing
shack. BILLIS *follows them in. After a few moments, he comes*
hurtling out, minus his wig. A few seconds later, the wig is
thrown out by one of the girls in the dressing room.

BILLIS

Oh, I beg your pardon.
  (*At this moment, he turns and faces* NELLIE, *who has*
  just come down the steps from the stage with another
  girl.)

NELLIE

(*Seeing* BILLIS)

Oh, Luther, you really are a honey-bun! These beautiful
flowers! I needed someone to think of me tonight. I appreciate it, Luther—you don't know how much.

BILLIS

(*Very emotionally*)

Miss Forbush, I would like you to know I consider you the
most wonderful woman in the entire world—officer and all.
And I just can't go on being such a heel as to let you think
I thought of giving you those flowers.

132

NELLIE

But you did give them to me and I—

BILLIS

(*Shoving a card at* NELLIE)

Here's the card that came with them. (*She reads the card, then turns away—deeply affected*) Are you all right, Miss Forbush? (*She nods her head*) I'll be waiting around the area here in case you need me. Just—just sing out.

(*He exits.* NELLIE *is on the point of tears.* CABLE, *who has been sitting on a bench below the ladies' dressing shack, now rises and approaches* NELLIE.)

CABLE

(*Sympathetically, but taking a light tone*)

What's the matter, Nellie the nurse? Having diplomatic difficulties with France?

(NELLIE *turns, startled.*)

NELLIE

(*Immediately becoming the professional nurse*)

Joe Cable! Who let you out of the hospital?

CABLE

Me. I'm okay.

(*She leads him to the bench and feels his forehead and pulse.*)

NELLIE

(*Accusingly*)

Joe! You're trying to get over to Bali Ha'i. That little girl you told me about!

CABLE

(Nodding thoughtfully)

Liat. I've just seen her for the last time, I guess. I love her and yet I just heard myself saying I can't marry her. What's the matter with me, Nellie? What kind of a guy am I, anyway?

NELLIE

You're all right. You're just far away from home. We're both so far away from home.

(She looks at the card. He takes her hand. EMILE enters. He is earnest and importunate.)

EMILE

Nellie! I must see you.

NELLIE

Emile! I—

EMILE

Will you excuse us, Lieutenant Cable?

(CABLE starts to leave.)

NELLIE

No, wait a minute, Joe. Stay. Please! *(To EMILE)* I've been meaning to call you but—

EMILE

You have asked for a transfer, why? What does it mean?

NELLIE

I'll explain it to you tomorrow, Emile. I'm—

EMILE

No. Now. What does it mean, Nellie?

NELLIE

It means that I can't marry you. Do you understand? I can't marry you.

EMILE

Nellie— Because of my children?

NELLIE

Not because of your children. They're sweet.

EMILE

It is their Polynesian mother then—their mother and I.

NELLIE

. . . Yes. I can't help it. It isn't as if I could give you a good reason. There is no reason. This is emotional. This is something that is born in me.

EMILE

(*Shouting the words in bitter protest*)
It is not. I do not believe this is born in you.

NELLIE

Then why do I feel the way I do? All I know is that I can't help it. I can't help it! Explain how we feel, Joe—
(JOE *gives her no help. She runs up to the door of the dressing shack.*)

EMILE

Nellie!

NELLIE

(Calling in)

Dinah, are you ready?

NURSE

Yes, Nellie.

NELLIE

I'll go with you.

> *(The other nurse comes out and they exit quickly.*
> EMILE *turns angrily to* CABLE.)

EMILE

What makes her talk like that? Why do you have this feeling, you and she? I do not believe it is born in you. I do not believe it.

CABLE

It's not born in you! It happens *after* you're born . . .

> (CABLE *sings the following words, as if figuring this*
> *whole question out for the first time*)

You've got to be taught to hate and fear,
You've got to be taught from year to year,
It's got to be drummed in your dear little ear—
You've got to be carefully taught!

You've got to be taught to be afraid
Of people whose eyes are oddly made,
And people whose skin is a different shade—
You've got to be carefully taught.

You've got to be taught before it's too late,
Before you are six or seven or eight,

To hate all the people your relatives hate—
You've got to be carefully taught!
You've got to be carefully taught!

(Speaking, going close to EMILE, *his voice filled with the emotion of discovery and firm in a new determination)*

You've got the right idea, de Becque—live on an island. Yes, sir, if I get out of this thing alive, I'm not going back there! I'm coming here. All I care about is right here. To hell with the rest.

EMILE

(Thoughtfully)

When all you care about is here . . . this is a good place to be. When all you care about is taken away from you, there is no place . . . *(Walking away from* CABLE, *now talking to himself)* I came so close to it . . . so close.

(Singing:)

One dream in my heart,
One love to be living for,
One love to be living for—
This nearly was mine.

One girl for my dreams,
One partner in Paradise,
This promise of Paradise—
This nearly was mine.

Close to my heart she came,
Only to fly away,
Only to fly as day
Flies from moonlight!

137

Now, now I'm alone,
Still dreaming of Paradise.
Still saying that Paradise
Once nearly was mine.

So clear and deep are my fancies
Of things I wish were true,
I'll keep remembering evenings
I wish I'd spent with you.
I'll keep remembering kisses
From lips I'll never own
And all the lovely adventures
That we have never known.

One dream in my heart
One love to be living for
One love to be living for—
This nearly was mine.

One girl for my dreams,
One partner in Paradise.
This promise of Paradise—
This nearly was mine.

Close to my heart she came,
Only to fly away,
Only to fly as day
Flies from moonlight!

Now . . . now I'm alone,
Still dreaming of Paradise,

Still saying that Paradise
Once nearly was mine.

(He drops to the bench, a lonely and disconsolate figure.)

CABLE

(Going to him)

De Becque, would you reconsider going up there with me to Marie Louise Island? I mean, now that you haven't got so much to lose? We could do a good job, I think—you and I. (EMILE *doesn't answer*) You know, back home when *I* used to get in a jam, I used to go hunting. That's what I think I'll do now. Good hunting up there around Marie Louise. Jap carriers . . . cargo boats . . . troopships . . . big game. *(He looks at* EMILE, *craftily considering how much headway he has made.* EMILE *smiles a little)* When I go up, what side of the island should I land on?

EMILE

The south side.

CABLE

Why?

EMILE

There's a cove there . . . and rocks. I have sailed in behind these rocks many times.

CABLE

Could a submarine get in between those rocks without being observed?

EMILE

Yes. If you know the channel.

CABLE

And after I land, what will I do?

EMILE

You will get in touch with my friends, Basile and Inato—two black men—wonderful hunters. They will hide us in the hills.

CABLE
(*His eyes lighting up*)
Us? Are you going with me?

EMILE
(*A new strength in his voice*)
Of course. You are too young to be out alone. Let's go and find Captain Brackett.

CABLE
(*Delirious*)
Wait till that old bastard Brackett hears this. He'll jump out of his skin!

EMILE

I would like to see this kind of a jump. Come on!
(*They go off quickly together.* BILLIS *rushes on and looks after them. Obviously, he's been listening. He thinks it over for a moment, "dopes it out." Then, with sudden decision, he takes one last puff on a cigarette butt, flings it away, and follows after them.*)

ACT TWO

Scene V

The lights go out and almost immediately the sound of an airplane motor is heard, revving up, ready for the take-off. The lights come up between the tapa-cloth and the dark-green drop.

Several Naval Aircraft mechanics are standing with their backs to the audience— They look off, watching tensely. As the plane is heard taking off, they raise their hands and shout in an exultant, defiant manner.

The music reaches a climax and the lights fade out on them, as they exit.

Lights in center come on simultaneously, revealing:

ACT TWO

Scene VI

This is the communications office or radio room. The back wall is covered with communications equipment of all sorts: boards, lights, switches. There is a speaker, a small table with a receiving set, various telephones and sending equipment. A COMMUNICATIONS ENLISTED MAN *is sitting at the table with earphones. He is working the dials in front of him.* CAPTAIN BRACKETT *is seated on an upturned waste basket. On the floor, are several empty Coca-Cola bottles and several full ones. He is eating a sandwich and alternately guzzling from a bottle of Coca-Cola. There are a couple of empty Coca-Cola bottles on the* ENLISTED MAN'S *desk, too.* BRACKETT *is listening avidly for any possible sound that might come from the loudspeaker. After a moment, there is a crackle.*

BRACKETT
(*Excitedly*)

What's that? What's that? (*The* ENLISTED MAN *cannot hear him, because he has earphones.* BRACKETT *suddenly becomes conscious of this. He pokes the* ENLISTED MAN *in the back. The* ENLISTED MAN, *controlling himself, turns and looks at* BRACKETT, *as a nurse would at an anxious, complaining patient. He pulls the earphones away from his ear*) What was that?

ENLISTED MAN
(*Quietly*)

That was . . . nothing, sir.

(*He readjusts his earphones and turns to his dials again.* BRACKETT, *unsatisfied by this, pokes the* ENLISTED MAN *again. The* ENLISTED MAN *winces, then patiently takes the earphones from his ears.*)

BRACKETT

Sounded to me like someone trying to send a message . . . sounded like code.

ENLISTED MAN

That was not code, sir. That sound you just heard was the contraction of the tin roof. It's the metal, cooling off at night.

BRACKETT

Oh.

ENLISTED MAN

Sir, if you'd like to go back to your office, I'll let you know as soon as . . .

BRACKETT

No, no, I'll stay right here. I don't want to add to your problems.

ENLISTED MAN
(*He turns back to his dials*)

Yes, sir.

(BRACKETT *impatiently looks at his watch and compares it with the watch on the* ENLISTED MAN'S *desk. He talks to the* ENLISTED MAN *who cannot hear him.*)

BRACKETT

We ought to be getting a message now. We ought to be getting a message, that's all. They'd have time to land and establish some sort of an observation post by now, don't you think so? (*He realizes that the* ENLISTED MAN *cannot hear*) Oh.

> (*He sits back in a position of listening.* HARBISON *enters. He is very stern, more upset than we have ever seen him.*)

HARBISON

Captain Brackett?

BRACKETT

Yeah, what is it? What is it? Don't interrupt me now, Bill. I'm very busy.

HARBISON

It's about this Seabee out here, sir, Billis! Commander Perkins over at Operations estimates that Billis' act this morning cost the Navy over six hundred thousand dollars!

BRACKETT

Six hundred— By God, I'm going to chew that guy's—send him in here!

HARBISON

Yes, sir.

> (*He exits.* BRACKETT *goes over and taps the* ENLISTED MAN *on the shoulder. The* ENLISTED MAN *removes earphones.*)

BRACKETT

Let me know the moment you get any word. No matter what I'm doing, you just break right in.

ENLISTED MAN

Yes, sir.

(*He goes back to his work.* BRACKETT *paces another second and then* BILLIS *enters, wary, on guard; his face is flaming red, his nose is a white triangle, covered with zinc-oxide. He wears an undershirt. His arms are red, except for two patches of zinc-oxide on his shoulders. He is followed by* LIEUTENANT BUS ADAMS *and* COMMANDER HARBISON, *who closes the door.*)

HARBISON

(*Pushing* BILLIS *in*)

Get in there! Captain Brackett, this is Lieutenant Bus Adams, who flew the mission.

BRACKETT

H'y'a, Adams.

ADAMS

Captain.

(BRACKETT *beckons* BILLIS *to him.* BILLIS *walks over to him slowly, not knowing what may hit him.*)

BRACKETT

One man like you in an outfit is like a rotten apple in a barrel. Just what did you feel like—sitting down there all day long in that rubber boat in the middle of Empress Augusta Bay with the whole damn Navy Air Force trying to rescue you? And how the hell can you fall out of a PBY anyway?

BILLIS

Well, sir, the Jap anti-aircraft busted a hole in the side of

145

the plane and—I fell through . . . the wind just sucked me
out.

BRACKETT

So I'm to understand that you deliberately hid in the bag-
gage compartment of a plane that you knew was taking off
on a very dangerous mission. You had sand enough to do
that all right. And then the moment an anti-aircraft gun
hit the plane you fell out. The wind just sucked you out . . .
you and your little parachute! I don't think you fell out,
Billis, I think you jumped out. Which did you do?

BILLIS

Well, sir . . . er . . . it was sort of half and half . . . if you
get the picture.

BRACKETT

This is one of the most humiliating things that ever happened to me. Adams, when did you discover he was on the
plane?

ADAMS

Well, sir, we'd been out about an hour—it was still dark,
I know. Well, we were flying across Marie Louise. The Jap
anti-aircraft spotted us and made that hit. That's when Luther
. . . er . . . this fellow here . . . that's when he . . . left the
ship. I just circled once . . . time enough to drop him a
rubber boat. Some New Zealanders in P-40s spotted him
though and kept circling around him while I flew across the
island and landed alongside the sub, let Joe and the Frenchman off. By the time I got back to the other side of the
island, our Navy planes were flying around in the air above
this guy like a thick swarm of bees. (*He turns to grin at*
HARBISON, *who gives him no returning grin. He clears his*

throat and turns back to BRACKETT) They kept the Jap guns occupied while I slipped down and scooped him off the rubber boat. You'd have thought this guy was a ninety-million-dollar cruiser they were out to protect. There must have been fifty-five or sixty planes.

BILLIS

Sixty-two.

BRACKETT

You're not far off, Adams. Harbison tells me this thing cost the Navy about six hundred thousand dollars.

BILLIS

(*His face lighting up*)

Six hundred thous . . . !

BRACKETT

What the hell are you so happy about?

BILLIS

I was just thinking about my uncle. (*To* ADAMS) Remember my uncle I was telling you about? He used to tell my old man I'd never be worth a dime! Him and his lousy slot machines. . . . Can you imagine a guy . . .

(*He catches sight of* HARBISON's *scowl and shuts up quickly.*)

BRACKETT

Why the hell did you do this anyway, Billis? What would make a man do a thing like this?

BILLIS

Well, sir, a fellow has to keep moving. You know . . .

147

you get kind of held down. If you're itching to take a trip to pick up a few souvenirs, you got to kind of horn in . . . if you get the picture.

BRACKETT

How did you know about it?

BILLIS

I didn't know about it, exactly. It's just when I heard Lieutenant Cable talking to that fellow de Becque, right away I know something's in the air. A project. That's what I like, Captain. Projects. Don't you?

HARBISON

Billis, you've broken every regulation in the book. And, by God, Captain Brackett and I are going to throw it at you.

ADAMS

Sir. May I barge in? My co-pilot watched this whole thing, you know, and he thinks that this fellow Billis down there in the rubber boat with all those planes over him caused a kind of diversionary action. While all those Japs were busy shooting at the planes and at Billis on the other side of the island, that sub was sliding into that little cove and depositing the Frenchman and Joe Cable in behind those rocks.

BRACKETT

What the hell do you want me to do? Give this guy a Bronze Star?

BILLIS

I don't want any Bronze Star, Captain. But I could use a

little freedom. A little room to swing around in . . . if you know what I mean. If you get the picture.

BRACKETT

Get out of here. Get the hell out of here!
(*Moving up after* BILLIS. BILLIS *flees through the door.*)

HARBISON

I'd have thrown him in the brig. And I will too, if I get the ghost of a chance.
(*Suddenly, the* RADIO OPERATOR *becomes very excited and waves his arm at* CAPTAIN BRACKETT. *We begin to hear squeaks and static from the loudspeaker and through it we hear* EMILE DE BECQUE'S *voice. Everyone on the stage turns. All eyes and ears are focused on the loudspeaker.*)

EMILE'S VOICE

—And so we are here. This is our first chance to send news to you. We have made contact with former friends of mine. We have set up quarters in a mango tree—no room but a lovely view. . . . First the weather: rain clouds over Bougainville, The Treasuries, Choiseul and New Georgia. We expect rain in this region from nine o'clock to two o'clock. Pardon? Oh—my friend Joe corrects me. Oh—nine hundred to fourteen hundred. And now, our military expert, Joe.

CABLE'S VOICE

All you Navy, Marine and Army Pilots write this down.
(ADAMS *whips out his notebook and writes it as* CABLE *speaks*)
Surface craft—nineteen troop barges headed down the bottle

neck; speed about eleven knots. Ought to pass Banika at about twenty hundred tonight, escorted by heavy warships. (BRACKETT *and* HARBISON *smile triumphantly*) There ought to be some way to knock off a few of these.

(CABLE'S *voice continues under the following speeches.*)

ADAMS

Oh, boy!
    (*He goes to door.*)

HARBISON

Where you going?

ADAMS

Don't want to miss that take off. We'll be going out in waves tonight—waves—
    (*He exits quickly.* BRACKETT *sits down on waste basket and opens another Coke.*)

BRACKETT

Sit down, Bill. (HARBISON *sits, listening intently.* BRACKETT *hands him a Coca-Cola.* HARBISON *takes it*) Here.

HARBISON

Thanks.

BRACKETT

You know what I like, Bill? Projects—don't you?
    (*Lights start to fade.*)

CABLE'S VOICE

(*Which has been continuing over above dialogue*)
As for aircraft, there is little indication of activity at the

moment. But twenty-two bombers—Bettys—went by at 0600, headed southwest. There was fighter escort, not heavy . . . They should reach—

> (*The lights are now off the scene, but another part of the stage is lighted, revealing a group of pilots around a radio set, being briefed by an* OPERATIONS OFFICER.)

ACT TWO

Scene VII

OPERATIONS OFFICER

Listen carefully.

EMILE'S VOICE

Ceiling today unlimited. Thirty-three fighters—Zeros—have moved in from Bougainville. Their course is approximately 23 degrees— Undoubtedly, heavy bombers will follow.

OFFICER

(*To pilots who are writing*)

Got that?

(*Lights out. Light hits another group.*)

NAVY PILOT

(*To a group of officers*)

Well, gentlemen, here's the hot tip for today. Joe and the Frenchman have sighted twenty surface craft heading southeast from Vella Lavella. Christmas is just two weeks away. Let's give those two characters a present—a beautiful view of no ships coming back.

AN OFFICER

Okay, that's all right with me.

(*They exit. Lights fade off and return to center of stage, revealing:*)

152

ACT TWO

Scene VIII

The Radio Shack again.
BRACKETT *is pacing up and down.* HARBISON *is standing near
the door, a pleading expression on his face.*

HARBISON

Sir, you just have to tell her something some time. She
hasn't seen him for two weeks. She might as well know it
now.

BRACKETT

Okay. Send her in. Send her in. I always have to do the
tough jobs.
> (HARBISON *exits. A second later,* NELLIE *enters, followed
> by* HARBISON. *She goes to* BRACKETT *and immediately
> plunges into the subject closest to her heart. Her speech
> is unplanned. She knows she has no right to ask her
> question, but she must have an answer.*)

NELLIE

Captain Brackett, I know this isn't regular. . . . It's about
Emile de Becque. I went to his house a week ago to . . .
You know how people have arguments and then days later
you think of a good answer. . . . Well, I went to his house,
and he wasn't there. I even asked the children . . . he has
two little children . . . and they didn't seem to know where

153

he'd gone. At least, I think that's what they said—they only speak French. And then tonight while I was on duty in the ward—we have a lot of fighter pilots over there, the boys who knocked out that convoy yesterday—you know how fighter pilots talk—about "Immelmanns" and "wingovers" and things. I never listen usually but they kept talking about a Frenchman—the Frenchman said this, and the Frenchman said that . . . and I was wondering if this Frenchman they were talking about could be—*my* Frenchman.

(*Pause.*)

BRACKETT

Yes, Miss Forbush, it is. I couldn't tell you before but . . . As a matter of fact, if you wait here a few minutes, you can hear his voice.

NELLIE

His voice? Where is he?

BRACKETT

With Lieutenant Cable behind enemy lines.

NELLIE

Behind . . . !

(*The* RADIO OPERATOR *snaps his fingers. All heads turn up toward the loudspeaker. They listen to* EMILE'S *voice on the radio.*)

EMILE'S VOICE

Hello. Hello, my friends and allies. My message today must be brief . . . and sad. Lieutenant Cable, my friend, Joe, died last night. He died from wounds he received three days ago. I will never know a finer man. I wish he could have told you the good news. The Japanese are pulling out and there is great confusion. Our guess is that the Japs will try to evacuate troops from Cape Esperance tonight. You may not hear from us for several days. We must move again. Two planes are overhead. They are looking for us, we think. We believe that . . . (*His speech is interrupted. There is the sound of a plane motor.* EMILE's *voice is heard shouting excitedly "off mike"*) What? . . . What? (*"In mike"*) Good-bye!

> (*There is a moment's silence. The* RADIO OPERATOR *works the dials.*)

BRACKETT

Is that all? Is that all? Can't you get them back?

RADIO OPERATOR

No, sir. They're cut off.

NELLIE

(*Tears in her eyes*)

Poor Joe. Poor little Joe Cable. (*She grabs* BRACKETT *and holds tightly to his arms*) Captain Brackett . . . Do you think there's a chance I'll ever see Emile de Becque again? If you don't think so, will you tell me?

BRACKETT

There's a chance . . . of course there's a chance.

NELLIE

(*Turning to* HARBISON)

I didn't know he was going.

BRACKETT

Of course not. How could he tell you he was going? Now don't blame Emile de Becque. He's okay . . . he's a wonderful guy!

(NELLIE *tries to answer, swallows hard, and can make only an inarticulate sound of assent.*)

NELLIE

Uh-huh!
(*She exits quickly.*)

BRACKETT

He has got a chance, hasn't he, Bill?

HARBISON
(*Hoarsely*)
Of course. There's always a chance!

BRACKETT

Come on! Let's get out of here!
(*Both exit, as the shack recedes upstage and a group of officers and nurses enter downstage to walk across the company street.*)

ACT TWO

Scene IX

The officers and nurses are singing the refrain of "I'm in Love with a Wonderful Guy."

NELLIE *walks on from the opposite side, looking straight ahead of her, a set expression on her face.*

NURSE
(As they pass her)
Coming to the dance, Nellie?
(NELLIE *just shakes her head and passes them.*)

A LIEUTENANT
What's the matter with her?
(Three girls in a trio and in a spirit of kidding NELLIE, *sing back over their shoulders at her, "She's in love, she's in love, she's in love, she's in love with a wonderful guy." Even before they have reached the end of this, the lights have started to dim. Now the lights come up in back, revealing:)*

ACT TWO

Scene X

The Beach.

NELLIE *walks on. The strain of "I'm in love, I'm in love, I'm in love" ringing in her ears and cutting deeply into her heart.* NELLIE *walks up and looks over the sea.*
Pause. Then she speaks softly.

NELLIE

Come back so I can tell you something. I know what counts now. You. All those other things—the woman you had before —her color . . . (*She laughs bitterly*) What piffle! What a pinhead I was! Come back so I can tell you. Oh, my God, don't die until I can tell you! All that matters is you and I being together. That's all! Just together— The way we wanted it to be the first night we met! Remember? . . . Remember?

    (*She sings*)
Some enchanted evening
When you find your true love,
When you feel him call you
Across a crowded room—
Then fly to his side,
And make him your own,
Or all through your life you may dream all alone . . .
    (*Music continues. She speaks*)

158

Don't die, Emile.

(*As the last line of the refrain is played,* BLOODY MARY *walks on and addresses* NELLIE, *timidly.*)

MARY

Miss Nurse! (NELLIE, *shocked by the sudden sound of an intruding voice, turns and emits a startled scream*) Please, please, Miss Nurse?

NELLIE

Who are you? What do you want?

MARY

Where is Lootellan Cable?

NELLIE

Who *are* you?

MARY

I am mother of Liat.

NELLIE

Who?

MARY

Liat. She won't marry no one but Lootellan Cable.

(LIAT *walks on slowly.* MARY *moves her forward and shows her to* NELLIE. NELLIE *looks at this girl and realizes who she is.*)

NELLIE

Oh. (NELLIE *rushes to her impulsively and embraces her*) Oh, my darling!

(*As she clasps* LIAT *in her arms, the noises of the company street burst harshly as the curtains close and we are plunged abruptly into:*)

ACT TWO

Scene XI

The company street is crowded with members of all Forces, ready to embark. There are sounds of truck convoys passing. Over the loudspeaker the following is heard:

VOICE ON LOUDSPEAKER

All right, hear this. All those outfits that are waiting for loading, please keep in position. We'll get to you as soon as your boat is ready for you.

(BILLIS, STEWPOT *and the* PROFESSOR *enter.*)

STEWPOT

Hey, Billis, let's head back, huh? Our gang's about a mile back down the beach. Suppose they call our names?

PROFESSOR

Yeah! They may be ready for us to go aboard.

BILLIS

They won't be ready for hours yet . . . this is the Navy. (*He turns and regards the scene offstage*) Eager Beavers! Look at that beach . . . swarmin' with 10,000 guys—all jerks! (*Picking out a likely "jerk"*) Hey, are you a Marine?

160

MARINE
(*Turning*)

Yeah!

BILLIS

Are you booked on one of those LCT's?

MARINE

I guess so, why?

BILLIS

They'll shake the belly off you, you know. (*He takes out a small package*) Five bucks and you can have it.

MARINE

What is it?

BILLIS

Seasick remedy. You'll be needing it.

MARINE

Aw, knock off! (*Pulls out a handful of packages from his pocket*) That stuff's issued. We all got it. Who are you tryin' to fool?

BILLIS
(*Turning to* STEWPOT)

These Marines are getting smarter every day.

OFFICER
(*Passing through*)

All right, all right. Stay with your own unit. (*To a nurse in combat uniform*) Ensign, you too. For Heaven's sake, don't get spread out over here. We're trying to get this thing organized as quickly as possible, so for God's sake, stay with your

161

outfit! (*To* BILLIS) Say, Seabee ... you belong down the beach.

BILLIS
(*Saluting officer*)
Excuse me, sir, could you tell me where we could find Captain Brackett?

OFFICER
He's up at the head of the company street. He'll be along any minute now.

BILLIS
(*Saluting*)
Thank you, sir. That's all, sir.
(*The* OFFICER, *having started off, stops in his tracks, stunned and rocked off his balance by being thus "dismissed" by* BILLIS. *Oh, well—too many important things to be done right now! He goes on his way, shouting:*)

OFFICER
All right! Stay in line! How many times have I told you ...
(*He is off. A* NURSE *comes by.*)

BILLIS
Hello, Miss McGregor. You nurses going too?

NURSE
Only a few of us. We're going to fly back some wounded.

BILLIS
Is Miss Forbush going with you?

NURSE

I don't know. She may be staying here with the hospital. (*She starts to leave.*)

BILLIS

Oh, Miss McGregor . . . you don't get airsick, do you? I was thinking maybe if you got three bucks handy, you might be able to use this little package I got here.

NURSE
(*Looking down at it*)
Oh, that stuff's no good . . . we gave that up last month.

BILLIS
(*Turning to* STEWPOT)
That's a female jerk! (BRACKETT *and* HARBISON *enter*) I beg pardon, sir . . . could I speak to you a minute?

BRACKETT
(*Peering through the semi-darkness*)
Who's that?

BILLIS

Billis, sir . . . Luther Billis.

BRACKETT

Oh. What do you want, Billis? We're moving out pretty soon.

BILLIS

Yes, sir, I know. I'd like to do something for Miss Forbush, sir. Stewpot and the Professor and me was wondering if anything is being done about rescuing the Frenchman off that island. We hereby volunteer for such a project . . . a triple diversionary activity, like I done to get 'em on there. You could drop us in three rubber boats on three different sides of the island . . . confuse the hell out of the Japs. . . . Get the picture?

BRACKETT

It's very fine of you, Billis . . . but you're too late for diversionary activity. That started this morning before the sun came up. Operation Alligator got under way. Landings were made on fourteen Japanese-held islands.

BILLIS

I think that's very unfair, sir. The first thing they should have done was try to rescue that Frenchman.

HARBISON

The Admiral agrees with you, Billis. Marie Louise was the first island they hit.

BILLIS

Did they get him? Is he alive?

BRACKETT

We don't know. Lieutenant Bus Adams flew up there to find out. He hasn't come back. But if the Frenchman's dead, it *is* unfair. It's too damned bad if a part of this huge operation couldn't have saved one of the two guys who made it all possible.

HARBISON
(*Gazing off*)

Look at the beach . . . far as you can see . . . men waiting to board ships. The whole picture of the South Pacific has changed. We're going the other way.

OFFICER

Captain Brackett, sir . . . the launch is ready to take you to your ship.

BILLIS

You got a ship, sir?

BRACKETT

Yes, Harbison and I've got a ship. I'm no longer a lousy Island Commander. Come on, Bill.

BILLIS

Good-bye, Commander Harbison.

HARBISON

Good-bye, Billis. Oh, by the way, I never did get you in the brig . . . did I?

BILLIS

(*Laughing almost too heartily at his triumph*)
No! Ha-ha.

HARBISON

Oh, I forgot!

BILLIS

(*Still laughing*)
Forgot what, sir?

HARBISON

Your unit'll be on our ship. I'll be seeing all of you.
(*Dismay from* BILLIS, STEWPOT *and the* PROFESSOR.)

BRACKETT

Come on, Bill.

(BRACKETT *and* HARBISON *exit.*)

OFFICER

(*Entering*)

All right . . . let's start those trucks moving out—all units on the company street. We're ready to load you. All Nurses will board assigned planes—Seabees to embark on Carrier 6. All Marines to board LCT's. Any questions? MOVE OUT!

(*The sound trucks roar. The music which has been playing under the scene mounts in volume. The men march off. Nurses in hospital uniform stand waving to the men and the nurses in combat uniform who leave with them. Soon the groups are all dispersed and lights come up in back, revealing:*)

ACT TWO

Scene XII

EMILE's *terrace.*

It is late afternoon. Sunset—reddish light. The drone of planes can be heard. JEROME *stands on a table.* NELLIE *holds him.* NGANA *is beside her. All look off.*

NELLIE

(Pointing off)

The big ones are battleships and the little ones are destroyers—or cruisers— I never can tell the difference. (*She looks up in the air*) And what on earth are those?

JEROME

P-40s.

NELLIE

Oh, that's right. They're all moving out, you see, because, well . . . there's been a big change. They won't be around here much any more, just off and on, a few of us. Did you understand anything I said? Vous ne comprenez pas?

NGANA

Oui, oui, nous comprenons.

(JEROME *nods his head.*)

167

JEROME

Oui.

NELLIE

Now, while I'm down at the hospital, you've got to promise me to mangez everything—everything that's put before you on the table—sur le tobler. Sur la tobler?

NGANA
(*Smiling patiently*)

Sur la table.

NELLIE
(*She smiles, congratulating herself*)

Now come back here, Jerome, and sit down. (*She starts to place the children at the table, on which a bowl of soup and some plates have been set. At this point,* BUS ADAMS *appears upstage—a weary figure. Behind him comes* EMILE *in dirt-stained uniform, helmet, paratroop boots and musette bag.* BUS *calls his attention to the planes droning above. Neither sees* NELLIE *or the children.* NELLIE *pushes the kids down, on the bench, as they playfully balk at being seated*) Ass—say—yay—voo. (*They sit.* EMILE *turns sharply at the sound of her voice*) Now you have to learn to mind me when I talk to you and be nice to me too. Because I love you very much. Now, *mangez.*

> (EMILE's *face lights up with grateful happiness.* BUS *knows it's time for him to shove off, and he does.* NELLIE *proceeds to ladle soup from the large bowl into three small bowls.*)

JEROME

(*His eyes twinkling mischievously*)
Chantez, Nellie.

NELLIE

I will not sing that song. You just want to laugh at my French accent. (*The kids put their spoons down—on strike*) All right, but you've got to help me.

NELLIE, NGANA AND JEROME

Dites moi
Pourquoi
   (NELLIE *is stuck. The children sing the next line without out her*)
La vie est belle.

NELLIE

(*Repeating, quickly, to catch up to them*)
La vie est belle.
   (*Meanwhile* EMILE *has crossed behind them.* NELLIE *is looking out front, not seeing him, trying to remember the lyrics, continues to sing with the children*)
Dites moi
Pourquoi . . .
   (*She turns to the children*)
Pourquoi what?
   (*She sees* EMILE.)

EMILE

(*Answering her, singing*)
La vie est gai!
   (NELLIE *gazes at him, hypnotized—her voice gone. The children rush to embrace him.*)

169

Dites moi
Pourquoi,
Chère mad'moiselle—

> (EMILE *leans forward and sings straight at* NELLIE.)

EMILE

Est-ce que
Parce que
Vous m'aimez—

> (*The music continues. The children drink their soup.*
> NELLIE *comes back to consciousness enough to realize*
> *that* EMILE *must be hungry. She leans over and hands*
> *him the large bowl of soup with an air of "nothing's-*
> *too-good-for-the-boss!" Then she passes him the soup*
> *ladle! But he doesn't use it. Instead, he thrusts his hand*
> *forward.* NELLIE *clasps it. Looking into each other's*
> *eyes, they hold this position as the curtain falls.*)